BRANDON FLORIDA	WATFORD HERTS
RIVERVIEW FLORIDA	CROXLEY GREEN HERTS
FORT POLK LOUISIANA	HARROW MIDDLESEX
FORT JACKSON SOUTH CAROLINA	LITTLE CHALFONT BUCKS
MANNHEIM GERMANY	RICKMANSWORTH HERTS
HARROW MIDDLESEX	SEATTLE USA
SHALSTONE BUCKINGHAMSHIRE	WEMBLEY PARK LONDON
RIVERVIEW FLORIDA	PINNER MIDDLESEX
DELTA AT TAMPA FLORIDA	CHORLEYWOOD HERTS
GRANTHAM LINCOLNSHIRE	LONGHOPE GLOUCESTERSHIRE
HAGWORTHINGHAM LINCOLNSHIRE	DELTA BC CANADA
GLEN ISLA SCOTLAND	SURREY BC
RUTHVEN SCOTLAND	LANGLEY BC
TAMPA FLORIDA	ABBOTSFORD BC
HAYSVILLE NORTHCAROLINA	SARDIS BC
LAKE NOTTELY GEORGIA	CHILLIWICK BC
HUDSON FLORIDA	HIGH RIVER ALBERTA
PLACIDA FLORIDA	NANAIMO VANCOUVER ISLAND
LITTLE GASPARILLA ISLAND FLORIDA	QUALICUM BEACH VANCOUVER ISLAND

Harrow Girls...Promises Kept

Harrow Girls...Promises Kept

Written by Lloyd Arthur Wiggins and
Rosemary Egerton Letts

Dedications:

To Nikki & John

Acknowledgments

We would like to thank: -

Our friends and relatives that helped to dig out old photos and jogged our memories.

Bill Carmen, Clare Carmen and Lyn Clayton for invaluable technical assistance and advice.

Jeff Jones for taking our photo.

Jim and Jeanette McGill for proof reading.

Susan Wade for proof reading.

Contents

Chapter 1

How It All Began

Ro's Story

Nineteen forty-six was the year Nikki and I were born. I was older by just three months. When we met, she had lived in Harrow, on Harley Crescent all her life. When my parents bought a house around the corner on Harley Road, I had no idea how fortunate that was. Even though we didn't become friends until we went to the same school three years later, our friendship would last nearly sixty years.

Nikki had such a magnetic personality and an enthusiasm for life. It was she who kept the Harrow group together through the decades, and she brought a lot of American friends into the fold. Now, all these years later, even without her here physically, we want to carry on her legacy by keeping in touch with each other and getting together whenever we can.

Because of the Second World War, our parents were in their late thirties when they had us, and we were only children. That gave us a special bond, and we grew up like sisters. Nikki might have been the younger one, but she had a lot more confidence than I did, and so with her I got to have a lot more fun than I would have otherwise had.

My mother, I learned later on, did not want children but was told by her doctor to have a child as it might cure a female problem she had. I always knew, though, that she loved me, and I certainly never felt unwanted. I was born in my uncle Maurice's bakery on March 6. We lived in the extra accommodations upstairs, and all went well until I started to toddle around. My earliest memory is of seeing a large tray of freshly baked Swiss rolls, and I remember considering whether to or not—but of course, I did. I put my finger in the middle of each one!

Shortly after that, we moved to a small house in Croxley Green that backed onto a canal. After several bouts of croup, the doctor advised that I should live somewhere less damp. Therefore we moved to 48 Harley Road when I was four. I remember standing outside of the house, holding my grandmother's hand and asking her, "Can we go home now nanna?" She replied, "Rosemary, you are home." And so it would be for the next fourteen years.

We had a dog named Dash that I was very close to. He was not the prettiest dog in the world, but he had a lovely nature. My mother told me she had seen him at the market as a puppy and he didn't have a single hair on his body. She felt so sorry for him that she brought him home. I'm sure Dash is one of the reasons why I have always loved dogs so much. We also had a cat called Luke, and Nikki had one called Mathew. Like me, she was a great animal lover and had many dogs and cats over the years. Nikki always supported local shelters wherever she lived.

My mother's sister, Joyce, had two little girls slightly older than me, Wendy and Rosalind. They could not say "Rosemary" so they called me "Ro Ro." The second Ro got dropped eventually, and that is why I am called Ro today.

**

It was January 1951 and my first day at St. Andrews School. It is still quite vivid in my memory. When my mother left me, I burst into tears. The teacher sat me in the desk next to Daphne Keeble, whom she thought would be a calming influence on me. She still is today, and we've been close friends ever since.

The walk from home up Hide Road to St. Andrews always seemed so long, but in fact it was only two blocks. St. George's Church was opposite the school, and that was where we went to Sunday school. I had to keep that a secret from all of my grandparents, as they were Christadelphians who did not accept the Church of England. My mum and dad had broken away from that religion in their twenties. St. Georges is the church where Daphne married Alan Dempster in 1963 and four years later Nikki married Lloyd Wiggins, but that is jumping ahead.

When we were seven, Daphne and I went to the secondary part of St. Andrews private school in North Harrow, which was a bus ride away. I think for financial reasons as well as convenience, Mum and Dad decided when I was nine, I should go to Bridge School where most of the neighbourhood kids went. It was within walking distance, coeducational, and there were no fees. It was here that I became friends with Veronica Hinch (Nikki), Jacque Bell, and Lynda Thompson, friendships that would last a lifetime. But I found Bridge School a bit rough after St. Andrews. There was a boy who would jump out and scare me on the last little stretch of Harley Road when I was walking on my own after saying goodbye to Nikki and Jacque at their homes on Harley Crescent.

That wasn't the only scare I got. One day when I was ten I was coming home from school, and as I approached the gate, I saw my mother lying in a pool of blood by the front of the house. She had fallen off the ladder while painting the trim. I will always remember that awful sight. I ran to the neighbors, and they called for an ambulance. Mum survived with a badly broken arm. She had to have a metal pin put in it but could never fully extend that arm.

We all enjoyed our summer holidays. When I think back to the freedom we had in those days! We were out all day, riding our bikes, going to the park, just showing up for meals. If the weather was bad, we'd be at each other's houses. Trips to the seaside were always fun. Mum and Dad made sure I had a friend along, even on the yearly two-week holiday. My dad loved driving and luckily always had a car provided with his job. He'd never taken a driving test because they were not required when he got his first license. Even though he never had an accident and always kept to the speed limit, no one that rode with him ever forgot the experience.

Soon I was eleven and my eleven-plus examination was approaching, and the pressure was on. The results determined which school you would go to. My mother, with best of intentions, started feeding me ProPlus caffeine tablets, thinking they would give me some kind of advantage. She also gave me an aspirin every night to help me sleep. Dad told me later that he would replace them with vitamin C tablets whenever he could!

The plan did not work. I remember overlooking complete pages of the exam papers, and when the dreaded results day came (big envelopes for fail, small ones for pass), needless to say I got the former. To make things worse for me, our dog, Dash, died at seventeen years old. He had been with me my whole life, and I was inconsolable.

Nikki and Jacque went on to grammar schools, and Lyn and I got sent to another private school, Harrow

College for Girls. It was run by two spinsters, Miss Pullun and Miss McKay. I'm sure it was a financial strain on my parents, but they thought it would give me the best chance of a good education.

Now I had to wear a school uniform and conform to a fairly strict code of conduct—always a challenge for me. However, I met some great girls there, and I enjoyed my time at Harrow College and did quite well in class despite my rebel ways. I have to give credit to my father, David Bailey Egerton, who always took time to make sure I "understood" what I was learning. How lucky was I to have him as my dad!

When I was twelve, Mum and Dad thought I should learn to ride. At the third lesson, the instructor put me on a large gray mare. I thought the horse looked awfully big, and I think it sensed my fear. Within just a few minutes, I was thrown to the ground. I'd put my left arm out to save myself, which resulted in a very bad fracture. The arm was set incorrectly, and to this day is quite crooked and one-and-a-half inches shorter than my right arm. Mum and I matched arms, and that was the end of my riding days.

Like all kids my age, friends were very important to me. I was still very close with Daphne, who lived at the top of Harrow View, a fifteen-minute walk away, but now I was spending more time with Nikki, who lived just around the corner, and Lynda, who lived on Walton Drive at the end of Harley Road. Pauline, who was in my class at school, was another only child, and we became great friends. She lived on Sudbury Court Drive, the other side of Harrow, a fifteen-minute bus ride away. I would often go for sleepovers at her house. Our parents socialized, and we went on several summer holidays together, usually to Butlin's Holiday Camp. One time, Pauline and I entered a talent contest in matching polka-dot dresses, and we sang, "Sisters, sisters—there were never such devoted sisters." Pauline and I had crushes on Marty Wilde and Cliff Richard, respectively. Marty Wilde still performs, and Pauline and her husband Cris go to see him whenever they can.

My mum's best friend was Enid, whom I always called Aunty. Her husband Sidney died very young, and after that Enid stayed with us every other weekend and became part of the family. Dad always took Enid and Mum a fancy breakfast in bed. That was very typical of his giving nature.

Mum and Dad were good friends with Nikki's parents, Flo and Jack, as well. Flo, who was manager of the United Dairies shop at the top of Harrow View, gave me my first job as Saturday help. One summer when I was fifteen, Daphne, Nikki, Lynda, and I were planning a hiking trip to the Lake District, staying in youth hostels. We had it all mapped out; we even got the equipment and supplies, etc. The Saturday before, at the United Dairies shop, I got a dreadful pain in my stomach, and Flo sent me home. No one was there, but I made it up to my bedroom. I'd never felt so ill. It seemed an eternity, but finally my parents returned and called an ambulance. It was acute appendicitis! Mum delayed in signing the forms because years before someone had used an unsterilized needle on her, in a similar operation, and it resulted in years of problems. The doctor, however, told her that I could die if not operated on soon. Luckily, I survived, but the hiking trip was canceled.

After being discharged from the army, in 1945 my father had become a commercial traveler in a number of different commodities. I particularly remember flour because he got his first slipped disc by lifting large bags of flour. Finally he found his forte in selling seeds and grains to farmers. Dad absolutely loved traveling the countryside in Buckinghamshire and Hertfordshire, and made many of the farmers his friends. When I was fully recovered, Dad arranged for us to camp in one of his farmer friend's fields for a few days as a small compensation for missing our hiking trip. We had fun in the tent. I remember Elvis on the radio singing "A Fool Such as I" and from that moment on, I was a fan. Poor Daphne got badly bitten by bugs, and I think we were all glad to be home in our own beds in the end.

One day, Nikki and I decided to walk from Harrow to Little Chalfont and back in one day. That was a thirty-mile hike, and we managed it, allowing ourselves two pieces of chocolate an hour. We were in bed for a few days after that recovering. We liked to go to the Petticoat Lane street market on Sundays and eat fruit on the way home on the train. Once I bought Dad a shirt there in a package, but when he opened it the body part was missing; it just had a front and collar.

Boys were part of our life now: walks in the park and going to the movies. Nikki and I went to a youth club in Harrow, and that was the start of the group that included David and Eddie Clayton and Dave Williamson, whom Nikki dated for a little while. We soon all realized we'd have more fun at each other's houses, so the get-togethers and the parties began. A different house each week, but I think we were at the Claytons' more than anywhere else. They were a lovely family, happy to see whoever dropped by. Our parents, too, were always glad for our friends to come over. They had their own great social life as well, so we often got the houses to ourselves. I remember one such weekend when mum and dad were away. I was sixteen or seventeen; so of course, with Nikki's encouragement I had a party. It wasn't too bad except that one of the boys drew in chalk all over the driveway that we shared with a neighbor, who was not impressed and duly complained to Mum and Dad. I believe the boy in question had to apologize to them. That was really as bad as it got.

Lynda and I had left Harrow College for Girls when we were fifteen and were now at Kilburn Polytechnic. We stuck together there, traveling up on the train, spending each lunchtime eating peas and chips at Lyon's Restaurant, and giggling in class at every opportunity. Neither of us knew what we wanted to do as a career; the choices seemed very limited back then. One day, I lost my geography folder, which contained hours of homework and study. I never went to geography class again!

Chapter 2

Poor Rural Florida Farm Boy

Lloyd's Story

I can remember back to the age of three, growing up with Floyd, my twin brother. We had our own gibberish language, and our mother and other siblings used to say they could not understand one word we were saying. Our gibberish ability seemed to fade once we started school. We would plan things out in the open, and then do something naughty that would end up in a switching for both of us. Sometimes our dad would scold or switch the wrong one of us since we were identical to him. This often happened later on in school when the teachers or the principal would call both of us in for a telling off or worse. Even our brothers and sisters were often wrong when trying to tell us apart. Mom was the only person who knew which one of us she was speaking to.

Every summer we were put in Bible School for two weeks at Providence Baptist Church; this we assumed was to give our mom a break. Snacks were always cookies and Kool-Aid. When we were too old for this, we were shipped off to a 4-H camp in the Ocala Forest, also for two weeks in the summer, along with other boys from Hillsborough County.

Uncle Wesley and Aunt Gertha were neighbors east of us on Bloomingdale Road. Gertha was dad's sister, and they also had a small, ten-acre farm. The neighbors west of us were Phil and Louise Simpson. They had two older boys, Gene and Jerry, and a younger daughter, Sharon. Mr. Simpson was a house builder, a rugged man who used to wrestle alligators, probably for a bet after a few in the tavern on the Alafia River in Riverview about five miles away, the closest town to where we lived.

Gene and his dad worked on Gene's racecar in their barn on weekends. Floyd and I would sneak over to see what they were doing. I remember at the age of four or five, we could not pronounce our *c*'s. Phil would say to us, after putting a piece of wood on his shoulder, "Now knock this chip off my shoulder." Then he would say, "Your turn, twins." Floyd put the piece of wood on his shoulder and said to Gene, "Knock this shit off my shoulder." Gene and his dad could not stop laughing. Of course, we were over there without permission and would always get caught. Gene was drafted and sent to the Korean War; to this day I remember how sad Mrs. Simpson seemed to be at church sometimes.

We were also always constantly in trouble with Uncle Wesley. I remember one time after a hard month of Wesley stringing barbed wire or hog wire between his farm and ours, Floyd and I climbed halfway up and started swinging, jumping, and pulling on the fence. He started running toward us. We were so scared; we ran home and dove under the far end of the bed so we couldn't be pulled out. Uncle Wesley worked for National Airlines at the airport. This was a very good job in the late 1940s and throughout the 1950s. Wesley bought a brand new Ford pickup, and we were caught trying to pour sand into the gas tank when he came over to show it to Mom and Dad. We really got a good hiding for that!

We all went to church at Providence Baptist three times a week. Our sister Prissy was put in charge of us one Sunday morning. Prissy being a very young teenager, this had all the makings of turning into an embarrassing chore. Floyd and I did not want to sit through one more boring sermon, so we both dove under the church. Prissy screamed at us to come out. Several of her peers joined her, and we both shouted back to her to go away. Well, we could not pronounce the *r* in Prissy—all we heard was *ugh!* And she threw up her hands in frustration of being called Pissy in front of everyone. Finally she asked a boy to crawl under the church to get us. She told off with some sharp words and finger wagging. Needless to say, Mom gave us a whipping in front of everyone at church.

In fact, Floyd and I got a switching daily. Mom would tell us to go in the side garden to find a stick to hit us with, and we would try to pick out the smallest stick or limb, usually of dried-out dog fennel, a weed that produces dry, bare sticks when dead. Then we would slightly break it where it couldn't be seen. It would break after the first or second hit. We would scream, "It hurts!" to make her stop or feel sorry for us.

By the age of six, Floyd and I wanted to play baseball, or hardball, as it was called in the 1950s, with our older brothers Fred and Avery and our cousin-to-be, Larry Trimble. We were going to have to wait another three years, which seemed like forever then. They all played during the summer at the Providence Park Community Center. The summers were so hot, and the water from the fountain was warm with sulfur smells and taste—it had an awful stench to it!

But even though we weren't old enough to play baseball, we finally got to ride the bus to school with the older kids. School was a disappointment, however. First grade at Riverview Elementary School was so boring, trying to write on that wide-lined paper. Our teacher, Mrs. Murphy, was a wonderful older lady, though, and we loved our classmates.

Our school was made out of wood and shaped like a large horseshoe with the principal's office at the top of the U. There was an open area in the middle, and all the classrooms were on the same level, seven steps up. When we were in second grade, spring was hot, and we had large sash windows always open for a breeze because there was no air-conditioning. One day I was sitting on the large windowsill and leaned back too far, falling ten feet to the ground and landing on my back. It was the first time I'd had the wind knocked out of me. The teacher thought it was curtains for me! That year went by quickly.

We loved not going to school in the summertime. In the summer of 1953, Floyd and I were given chores and we started to learn how to milk the cows. Our fingers were weak, hurting, trying to squeeze the milk out, but we could feed the chickens, hogs, and cattle just fine.

Our third-grade teacher looked like the witch from *The Wizard of Oz*. She always wore black and carried a yardstick for pointing and hitting. Floyd and I were in the principal's office for a paddling at least once a week. We never told our parents because that would have gotten us another paddling at home. Once the teacher caught me flicking spitballs and sent me to the principal's office. This was the first time that I stuck a soft thin book inside my underwear to thwart the paddle—it worked! I did not mind the paddlings after that.

That Christmas, Wayne Pierce, who sat next to me, got a silver chain to wear around his neck. It looked so trendy! That year we had indoor plumbing put in for the bathroom, and the chain for the bath plug looked the same as Wayne Pierce's chain. Since I was color-blind it was good enough for me. I wore it to class in January, and Wayne said out loud that I was wearing a bathtub chain. This was the first time I was ever embarrassed in front of anyone.

After third grade When we were nine we were finally allowed to play baseball in the summertime. Mr. Summerall was our coach and his son Larry, was on the team. This same group would go hunting or camping most Friday nights. One time, the whole team went camping on Lake Thomas. Everyone was swimming except Floyd and me. We were not good swimmers. They all picked us up, took us to the middle of the lake, and then threw us in to either sink or swim. We learned to swim quickly.

After the summer was over, we were back planting crops or feeding and milking the livestock. At night all of us took turns weaving cast nets. Dad would sell them by special orders of different lengths. When the peas were ready, we spent time shelling them to sell and be canned. We had to be in bed by eight thirty so we could wake up at four thirty in the morning to feed or milk the livestock and catch different buses to elementary or high school.

It was nineteen sixty one and every day after school, we had to hoe cane, peas, and beans and mend fences. Dad worked two jobs, and Avery worked at the *Tribune/Times* with him. Fred had just started there too, Therefore every job on the farm was left to Floyd and me. Ninety percent of our daylight hours were spent working, and our pay, we were told many times, was food, clothing and shelter. We never did get any allowance like other children. We would get twenty-five cents a day for school lunches, and we would skip lunch two days a week so we could have some jingle in our jeans.

I remember one time Floyd and I skipped school and went to the Alafia River to swim all day. That afternoon we waited for the bus to show up at our home bus stop so we could come out of the tall weeds and pretend we were at school. I'm glad Mom and Dad never found out. We were still getting whippings, usually from Dad's belt since we were getting to be taller than Mom.

Floyd and I did everything together, but in sixth grade I had a girlfriend I did not want to share. Her name was Josette. Her parents owned a fruit and vegetable stand, and Josette would slip me notes and letters just before I boarded the school bus for home. They were sprayed with perfume, and Floyd always wanted to read them, so I had to stash them in the wall of our bedroom where there were gaps in the pine boards. It was very cold in the winters with no insulation or heat and no doors on any of the children's bedrooms. We all had to double up in the beds since we were eight children in all.

At the start of the next school year, there were so many students that the class had to be split into two classes. The principal was calling out the names to form a line for Mrs. Johnson's class. Mrs. Johnson was a beautiful blond, about five-foot-one and slightly built. The other teacher was tall and mean looking. Floyd's name was called, but he was talking to Brady and did not hear. Not wanting Floyd to get into trouble, I joined Mrs. Johnson's line.

Three weeks later on the bus home, Floyd asked if I knew he was supposed to be in Mrs. Johnson's class. I said I was protecting him from a visit to the principal's office that he should have thanked me. I liked that class so much that my grade average was a B. Floyd's was a C-. Teachers really do make a difference.

**

Our sister Clara was the angel out of all of us. No one ever knew she was around; she was so quiet and always doing chores for Mom or studying for school. Clara was always volunteering to do Floyd's and my chores so we could play or practice baseball at the local park. God, how I loved her.

When she was fourteen, Clara got sick and passed away. While she was sick, Floyd and I were farmed out to Aunt Billie (my mom's sister) and Uncle Gordon. They lived on a large orange grove, and Gordon worked for the railroad along with their son Jimmy. Their other son, Jackie, was in his senior year at Brandon High School. We were treated very well, but however nice they were to us, we were still homesick, longing to play football with our brothers and neighbors. I flunked that year of school.

Christmas was always special in our family, but when Clara left to go home to heaven, there was no tree or presents that year. Floyd and I went out on the farm to find a tree. We found a small pine, dug it up, and took to the house. We hung tinsel on our tree, but how sad that Christmas was. You never know how much you love someone until they are no longer with you. I regret not telling her so. Clara is always in my prayers with thanks and love for all she meant to us. She was my guardian angel and still is. I just feel her presence, especially later in life.

The next year was empty without Clara, but our new brother was born in September. He was a *BIG* surprise. This helped a little for Mom and Dad and he of course, received all of the attention.

We could not wait to go to high school! Graduating from elementary school was nothing special in our family, but Floyd and I were still happy to leave Riverview Elementary. Our happiness was soon over. Monday we were back to work, tractoring, hoeing, and bailing hay, stacking it in the barn.

It seemed every summer was extremely hot, working in the fields or on the tractor for hours on end—and not only our fields! The neighbors needed the earth turned over with a disk. When Floyd or I was running the tractor, the other had to break up the clods. The only respite from the heat was a long swim in the Alafia River. Since we had to sneak off to avoid being seen, we would have to go through Aunt Gertha and Uncle Wesley's farm running like a couple of convicts trying to get away from the chain gang. We knew the river was at least a twenty-minute run, and to be gone an hour was pretty safe.

Our parents banned us from quite a few local activities including swimming. The most puzzling was at Larry Summerall's birthday party one summer evening. We had to climb out of our bedroom window to go it; needless to say we were caught crawling back into the window an hour later. The whipping was worth it all. We were really getting tired of being restricted. There was no hope of ever having a car; we were not even allowed a bicycle all those years. Both of us knew that the chance of having a normal teenage life in the future was remote, as long as our parents needed someone to do all the feeding and milking the livestock.

We finally were on our way to East Bay High School. The school was so large that finding our way around was daunting. The older boys were always bullying the freshmen, some a lot more than us. In the ninth grade, Floyd and I were very quiet. The principal was a tall, dark, tanned man, and his opening remarks at the start of school were "I give you fair warning not to cross the line." He seemed to start off every student gathering with these words.

We both selected the same schedule, which included Drivers Ed. It was such a great feeling, being old enough to do something older people did. I will never forget the instructor being so patient and wanting everyone to do well. Future Farmers of America (FFA) was our second-favorite course.

Deacon Jones, our teacher, was a short, wiry guy with hair like Glen Campbell, and he wore cowboy boots all the time.

We wanted to participate in organized sports. Our baseball talents had been honed in the community parks of Hillsborough County, but our best chance would have been on the track team in pole vault since we had a pole-vault pit on the farm. We used bamboo poles while the school had aluminum poles, which were much safer. However, our parents told us our chores were too important for us to engage in any school activities. This meant no dances, no girlfriends, no cars, and no freedom to hang out with the other students on weekends and holidays.

However, FFA had an initiation night on a Friday, and our parents let us go! What crazy fun! We new freshmen were blindfolded and our hands thrust into a pail of goo with worms. That was all there was; we all pretended to be grossed out, but living on a farm with cattle or chickens, you either stepped or fell in much worse.

Entering the tenth grade was really going up in the hierarchy of students at East Bay High School. That year, Deacon Jones started early talking about exhibiting livestock at the Florida State Fair in Old Tampa. He also talked about exhibiting at the Strawberry Festival in Plant City with the same livestock.

Floyd and I went home and told Dad about the chance to show the livestock and sell them at the last fair, usually to large, local companies for their advertising. Dad agreed to buy two Black Angus steers for the chance of selling them at an inflated price.

In AG we were taught how to mix feed so the steers would put on weight. We only had from September to February to get them ready and heavy. They had to be trained to be led into an arena for judging. They also had to be tamed so judges could poke them for fat or firmness. Early on we tried to teach them to be led, but they were very stubborn. After weeks of trying, I told Floyd, "Let's hook them up to the tractor!" We led them by tractor, and since the tractor was forceful, they gave up being so stubborn.

In February 1963, we took the steers to the Florida State Fair with Dad and Deacon Jones. We set them up in their own pen with bales of hay. Then we were told that we had to stay with them all night! But it turned out to be fun. We met with the other FFA and 4-H Club exhibitors. Some played guitars and sang Western songs; all of us had working cowboy hats.

We were nervous going into the arena the next day. Everything went well, and we got ribbons for grooming. We probably groomed those steers for at least two hours before showing them. We also got ribbons for leading skills. Then we headed back to the farm to get ready for the Strawberry Festival. This was where the two steers were going to be sold. It was one more week of heavy feeding and washing plus grooming.

Our two Angus steers performed brilliantly. Floyd's steer did better than mine: his got $1.10 per pound and mine got $1.01 a pound. Since they both topped one thousand pounds, in 1963 that translated into a load of money! Mom and Dad were ecstatic! Floyd and I asked what would our share be and were told that being clothed, fed, and sheltered was our share. We were shattered since we had trained and fallen in love with these two magnificent animals. We did not know then, but it was to be the beginning of the end of this type of life, which was unpaid arduous labor, under our parents rule.

The rest of 1963 was hard. AG class was always fun, but the only enjoyment at home was to practice our pole-vaulting whenever we could. Every once in a while, Dad would take us cast netting for mullet over by the Sunshine Causeway. We had to sit under the bridge until we caught something. At sixteen years old, we found this very boring.

That summer was hot again. Harvesting, grinding, cutting, and cooking cane for syrup was a lot of work. Dad put the syrup into gallon cans to sell. We were glad to see the end of the cane, but we still had to bale the hay. We also got a job at Bishop's Dairy baling and stacking hay for one week. Another job was mending fences for Angie and Art Draper for $1.25 an hour. I also worked part-time that summer for Mr. Pratt and his son Gene. Mom and Dad said that we could buy our own clothes for school that year since we worked for others between doing our own chores. What a life of drudgery that was! I think Dad was getting meaner; who knows what went on in his mind.

Summer was finally over and we started the eleventh grade. AG class started with the officers being elected. Floyd was elected as alderman; I remember wishing I had run for something so it could be stitched into the front of my FFA jacket. I loved that gold and dark blue blazer.

Nineteen sixty-four was much the same—work, school, church. Dad did relent and let us go out for the track team with one provision: we did not go out for the pole-vaulting team. Our older brother Fred had attempted a twelve-foot jump, and the bamboo pole broke; he had a bad concussion and could not say or respond to anything for thirty minutes. However, pole-vaulting was the only thing Floyd and I were good at on the track team, so we lied to Dad and told him we were runners.

Dad said we had to hitchhike home every day and we had better be home to do the chores. It was a long, long way to hitchhike. After the fourth track meet, Dad came to see us compete. He took us away after he saw us pole-vaulting—oh my, what else could go wrong? We got a whipping when we got home.

One Sunday evening in late March, Dad must have heard us talking on the way home from church about how much we wanted to pole-vault and how unfair it was that we weren't allowed to go to junior prom. When we got home, we could hear him walking down the hallway as he drew his belt through the belt loops on his trousers.

Floyd was the first one out of bed to meet him at the doorway. He said, "The beatings are stopping tonight."

Dad said, "It's either the belt or the fist." Then he swung at Floyd. Thank God Floyd moved out of the way! I was thinking I could take the belt; it didn't show outside of our clothes. Dad turned away and went back to his room.

Lloyd & Floyd 5 years old, Riverview

Nikki 1952

The twins 7 years old

The twins with their mom Cassie 3 years old

Nikki & Ro playing tennis, 13 years old

Nikki & Ro in the snow, Harley Road, 1959

Chapter 3

London in the Sixties

Ro's Story

I left Kilburn Poly after a year and went to Cheswick
Technical College to take a hairdressing course. There was
a pattern immerging here of not sticking to one thing for
very long. After that course, my mother came with me for
an interview at Harrods department store for a three-year
apprenticeship, for which I was accepted. It was 1963 and I
was seventeen. There were twenty-one apprentices in this
huge hairdressing department and about the same amount
of qualified stylists. It was hard work, but we had lots of
fun. There were two large, open salons and about twenty-
five individual rooms where it was easy to sneak away to
do each other's hair and makeup. We learnt to do hot
permanent waves with the curlers were wired in, and they
got extremely hot! Quite a few celebrities came there, and I
remember serving them tongue sandwiches and hot Bovril
among other things. The wage was minimal £2.34 a week,
but being at Harrods made it worth it. My dad was teaching
me to drive at this time, so I would drive his car with him to
Rayners Lane Station and then ride the Tube with Linda
Merritt and Carol Snowden, friends and fellow apprentices.
Fashion and music were very important to us; after all, it
was London in the sixties with Twiggy and the Beatles.

I realize now how lucky I was to have been a teenager at that time in history and working in London. On occasion, instead of staying on the train to Knightsbridge, Carol and I would get off at Oxford Street and go to the sales. On another occasion, we got into the department very early in the morning after our all-night party and caught a couple hours of sleep on the beauty beds. Somehow we got away with it!

Nikki was my main model and was always such a good sport. She never got upset when things went wrong. One day, up in my bedroom, I turned her hair orange and then green. I ended up giving her a drastic haircut and we just laughed and laughed.

The day of my driving test arrived. I was still seventeen and I felt enormous pressure to pass because my dad had taught me, and I wanted him to be proud. As nervous as I was, I somehow held it together enough to pass the test. I remember rushing home so happy and relieved; however, within a few hours, I was covered in a nervous rash all over my body.

Something else that made my seventeenth year memorable was a holiday to Jersey with Nikki for a week. We could not believe our parents let us go—we were so excited. It was a party place, and we partied! Herman's Hermits, "I'm Into Something Good," was playing on the radio. Whenever I hear it I remember that Jersey holiday.

Meantime, Daphne had met Alan Dempster; they matched perfectly, both with a wicked sense of humor, so it was no surprise when they decided to get married. She was seventeen and he was five years older, fresh from the Navy. Daphne asked me to be her bridesmaid and do her hair. It was a beautiful wedding, the first one of our group, but because I had just broken up with a boy called Andy (who always wore sunglasses indoors, which I thought odd) I felt a little jaded.

My grandfather had died recently, and it was decided that Mum and Dad should sell the house on Harley Road and move in with my grandmother in her chalet bungalow in Little Chalfont, Buckinghamshire. She was not well and needed looking after. I hated to leave Harrow and all my friends, but it was not that far away, and a lot of us were driving. My grandfather left me two hundred pounds, and with a little extra from Mum and Dad, I bought an Austin A35.

I had been at Harrods for eighteen months out of a three-year apprenticeship, but because of the time and travel expense from Little Chalfont to Knightsbridge, it made sense to transfer the apprenticeship to somewhere more local. I left Harrods and started at "Francis and Elizabeth," a hairdressing salon in the village of Gerrards Cross. Everyone was very nice and I enjoyed making more new friends, especially Heather Plain. Mr. Pierce, my boss, got me doing manicures, too, without any formal training, but I managed to wing it and enjoyed the tips.

In December of 1964, Lynda Thompson persuaded me to go on a blind date with herself and John Letts, whom she had met while on holiday. John was at London University and had a friend from the Canary Islands. It went quite well, but I knew nothing serious was going to come of it. On January 2, 1965, Lyn rang me up: she was in a predicament. She had agreed to go to Nikki's party with a boyfriend called Dave, and John Letts had called her to say he was in town—so could I take John, just platonically. I remembered he was a very nice, quiet guy so I said, "Sure, I'll do it."

I had a great sense of anticipation that night, getting ready and driving to Lyn's place where we were all going to meet. I wore a pale gray dress with ruffles around the neck, and when John walked in he had on a green corduroy jacket. I thought he looked so handsome. Anyway, we agreed that when we got to the party we would go our separate ways. We did for a short while, but the attraction between us was too strong. We spent the evening together and in the morning woke up together in an armchair.

John said he would drive me back to Little Chalfort in my car, but I insisted on driving, wanting to show off, I suppose. It was icy that morning, and after only a few miles I suddenly skidded on Roxborough Bridge and hit a Vauxhall head-on! Both cars sustained a fair bit of damage, but luckily, we were all able to drive away.

I arrived home on that Sunday morning with a strange boy and a dented car after having been out all night! My mother was in bed with a slipped disk, and my poor dad was as angry as I've ever seen him. Little did he realize that before long he would love John like the son he never had. The crash with the Vauxhall ended up costing me twenty-one pounds in labor (plus parts), which was a fortune back then, as I was still earning less than three pounds a week.

The next few months were magical. John and I were in love, phoning and writing letters every day. We lived for the weekends, either in London, on Little Chalfont, or in Harrow. I remember walking around London together. We would go to different, posh restaurants and share an appetizer together, often mushrooms on toast. We would leave the money on the table and rush out before they realized we were not having a main course.

Nikki had gone to a teachers training college in Eastbourne on the south coast, and she was not happy there, missing Harrow and all her friends. In February she managed to get a transfer to a London college as a day student. I was so happy, and we got back to playing tennis, trying new hair colors or going to the pub with the group. I was a cheap date, only drinking pineapple juice most of the time as I couldn't handle alcohol. Nikki, on the other hand, being Nikki loved her Pims number one and could manage several! It made the weekdays without John much more bearable. Nikki's driving wasn't much better than mine, and one night, trying to leave a friend's house, she backed straight into another friend's new Mini; then she moved forward, let the handbrake off, rolled back, and hit it again! The poor boy just stood and watched it happen.

On April 10, Daphne had a baby boy, Steven Paul. We were all very happy for her and Alan. They were the first of our group to get married and to have a child. They continued that way through life, being the first grandparents and great grandparents.

John was struggling with his studies at London University. He was living in a bedsit on his own with piles of work ever mounting; it did sound depressing. He was on the verge of quitting when we met, and somehow, I inspired him to carry on.

John's twenty-first birthday was May 26. I gave him gold cufflinks, and we went to town for a meal and celebrated. John proposed at a pub in Putney on June 2, and of course I accepted! I will always remember that I was wearing a pink suit and had greenish hair (ash blond that had gone wrong). We planned to get officially engaged the following September, when John would have saved enough to buy a ring. (He later bought the engagement ring in Harrow at the same jewelers where, unknowingly, Lloyd bought Nikki's ring the following year.) Nikki and Lyn were thrilled when I told them the news the next day.

John's exams finished on the seventeenth of June, and on the eighteenth I helped him move out of his digs. We had a few days before he was due to go back to Paignton,

Devonshire, to work as a waiter at the same hotel where he had met Lyn the year before. My mum treated us to a farewell meal at the Greyhound Pub. We were both dreading the separation, but he needed the money. No more weekends, just daily letters and phone calls, missing each other like crazy. John took on an extra job as wine waiter to fill in the time and earn a bit more money. I filled my time by doing hair and playing tennis. By mid-July we were both desperate to see each other, so he called me to say he was coming home. I'll never forget the day I met him at the bus stop in Southall: Saturday, July 17, 1965. It was with incredible excitement and emotion—that feeling of being so in love, your heart is bursting.

On July 22 we heard that John had passed his exams—marvelous news! The next day John got a job at Dewhurst Electrical Fitters at a wage of eleven pounds a week. In the evening we went to Ed Clayton's twenty-first birthday party. John was able to enjoy playing golf again after all that studying. One Saturday evening in August, we motored down to Bognor Regis in my A35 car, swam in the sea, and drove back. We got home at one a.m.

John found a really good deal for a two-week holiday in Majorca. Now that we were going to get engaged, Mum and Dad were OK with the idea, and we couldn't wait to be alone together for two whole weeks. We had a glorious time, but we really had to eke the money out, as we had to buy water, which we had not expected. We were just happy to have each other, the sun, and the sea. When we got home, Mum and Dad threw us an engagement party and all of the friends came. It was the best of times.

Chapter 4

Off to the Army

Lloyd's Story

The next day, Floyd talked me into going to Tampa to the army recruiter to join the army. The recruiter gave us a test; we passed, but he said our parents would have to sign us up.

We asked if both parents had to sign, and he said, "No, just one."

Floyd said, "Our dad works in Tampa for the *Tribune*. Can we take it to him and return it later today?"

He said, "Sure."

So we went outside, forged his signature, and thirty minutes later returned it to the sergeant. He asked us when we wanted to go. We said that week, but he told us the next trip was the next Monday to the Jacksonville Naval Station Induction Center. We said fine, we would wait until then.

We had skipped school that day and had to hitchhike home. At school the next day, we told all of our teachers that we had enlisted. They were upset, especially our AG teacher, Deacon Jones, who tried to talk us out of it. We told him that life at home was never going to change, and I think he understood. That Friday we told Mom and Dad that we were off to the army on Monday. Dad's only reply was "You boys are going to find out what tough is." I believe, though, that they really were taken aback.

That weekend was a blur, not knowing what to expect at the induction center. I remember going up by bus on Monday and on Tuesday standing in line with at least fifty other recruits, stripped down to our underwear, examined, poked, prodded, and shot with needles. The next day was exams. After the induction center formalities, Floyd and I were told along with many others that Fort Jackson was full and we were to be flown to Alexandria, Louisiana, for boot camp at Fort Polk.

Wow! What a place Fort Polk was. Out in the middle of thicket, swamps, and pine forest, we had never seen coal fireplaces before. The mornings started off with calisthenics and a three-mile run before breakfast, singing rhythmic songs to keep us all in step. We were told our boot camp would go to the woods camping for one week at the most. Our second week, we were trucked to our first bivouac and had instruction on nerve gas and also chlorine. Then we went into the tear gas tent with masks on. You could see the fumes coming out of the pots. When we were all inside, we were instructed to take our masks off. I could not stand the burning and stinging, but I had to keep my mask off and recite the Military Code of Conduct. After another five minutes, we were told to go outside, twenty soldiers at a time, looking for water to splash on our faces. The next day we went back to the barracks.

We started training for the physical training proficiency exam. There were five disciplines including dodge and jump and grenade throwing with duds. They were heavy grenades, too heavy to throw like a baseball. And there was also the bayonet course. We started training on the parallel bars, twenty-five bars long, and for a one-mile run with combat boots, backpack, and weapon, which had to be completed in less than eight minutes for the maximum of one hundred points.

We only had another six weeks to master the exercises. Since Floyd and I had been on the East Bay track team, the three running events were easy. After evening mess, if time permitted, Floyd and I would go to the parade grounds to practice on the parallel bars. It didn't take long to realize that you had to get a rhythm going by swinging your body toward the next bar. Within days, we had easily mastered it. But since all of the guys had to go at the same time, you only had one chance. If you started and fell to the ground, you had to get out of the way before the next soldier was on his way.

By the time the third week had ended, we were homesick, even as bad as we thought home was. I would pray that this turned out to be a nightmare and I just wake up, do my chores, and go to school. A lot of young men in our platoon felt the same way.

The fourth weekend we were allowed to go to the base PX (the army store) and bar. Since we didn't drink, we both had Fire Guard which is a one hour exercise walking around the barracks throughout the night with a baseball bat under our ponchos. One soldier, an American native whose last name was Peek, was close enough to the perimeter that I shouted, "Halt! Who goes there?" He didn't answer and came up to me in a threatening manner. I shoved the bat into his stomach. I did not know our sergeant, who was as black as the night, was lying in the ditch only yards away. He took Peek to the ground and dragged him by the chin to the captain of the guard. That really shook me up, thinking someone could sneak up without me knowing it.

The fourth week we went out to the woods and camped for three nights. We had night training with infrared goggles, then marched back to the barracks to finally shower and get some sleep. The next morning we were up at six a.m. for exercises and the three-mile run. We usually stopped at the mess hall at the end, but this particular morning, we ran another three miles. When we got back to the mess hall, the sergeant asked us,

"Are you girls ready to stop?"

We all said in unison, "*No sir!*" We were going to run this S.O.B. into the ground!

After our ninth mile, he asked again, "OK, girls. Do you want breakfast?"

We all said in unison, "*Yes sir!*" I guess he won; however, we finally came together as a team.

**

Our fifth week was a thirty-mile march to the rifle range we would call home for the next seven days. That first day, we marched for twenty-five miles; then we were told to pitch our tents in the dark for supper, and we also had a mail call. Before we had time to read any of our mail, we were told to break camp; it was now eight thirty at night in pitch-black darkness. I could not believe we were going on. We marched only another five miles, but it seemed like it was midnight when we finally arrived on the outskirts of the range.

The next morning we were all dragging at breakfast, and then we got into formation to march to the rifle range. It took five days to qualify everyone. We all had to take our turns in the pits, patching targets. This was a dreadful job, slapping glue and squares of paper to cover the bullet holes. Then we had to hold up either a black flag for a bull's-eye or a red flag called Maggie's Drawers when a bullet missed the target. This procedure took forever after every shot. We each had to qualify every hundred yards up to five hundred yards in both prone and standing positions. The drill instructor would yell out, "Ready on the right. Ready on the left. Ready on the firing line!" No wonder this took five days and one day on each end to march to and from the barracks.

The sixth week was mostly classroom lectures on bleachers at the parade ground for three days and then back to the woods for two days. This was only a fifteen-mile march on a wooded path. We were "bombed" by fighter planes with one-pound flour sacks. If the white flour got on you, it was considered a kill. After a few more miles, we were told to take a mock Viet Cong encampment, and we were given blanks to shoot up the enemy. Now this was very exciting.

During the seventh week of basic training, we were back to getting ready for the end of the physical exams. On that Thursday morning at one a.m., we were rousted from our bunks and told to be in formation in ten minutes in front of the barracks. Cattle trucks were brought in to transport us to who knew where with weapons strapped to our shoulders. We boarded the trucks, and they drove for some thirty minutes back into the woods. How big was this army base? We stopped at a chain link fence with barbed wire. No buildings, this was infiltration training. We had to do a low crawl and back crawl for one hundred yards, through water-filled trenches with barbed wire one foot above our crawling bodies. We were told it was a contest to see who could get to the other side first. We were also told, by no means, not to stand up or get up on our knees or we would be killed.

We all started and so did the machine gun fire. Every sixth bullet was a tracer which is a bullet illuminated with phosphorus. Bunkers with banked-up sandbags filled with explosives were going off, shaking the ground around us. After it was all over, we were transported back to the barracks. We were covered in sand and mud; our rifles were uselessly caked with mud. We all hit the showers with our rifles. I had dirt in my ears, up my behind, up my armpits, everywhere! We also washed our rifles. By this time it was six a.m. and we had to break our weapons down, dry every piece, then oil every piece, then wipe the excess oil away so it would not attract too much lint. We finally made it to the mess hall around eight a.m. The rest of that Thursday we were back into lectures on the parade ground. The next four days were spent preparing for the big test.

On test day, the commanding officer had a meeting with Floyd and me. He said if we scored a perfect five hundred we would have a write-up in the army news. In the first four events we scored the max: four hundred. Then Floyd scored a seventy-seven on the grenade throw. My score was approximately eighty-six. The old man was a little disappointed.

Next was graduation, then home for a two-week furlough before showing up for advanced infantry training at Fort Jackson in South Carolina. Our brother Fred picked us up at the Tampa Airport. When we got home, all we heard from Dad was, again, "You boys have no idea how hard it's going to be." We kept quiet; we had come through "hard" and stayed the course.

**

After two weeks in Florida, Floyd and I flew to Fort Jackson. We chose a transportation school because we both loved to handle cars and trucks. We were trained on jeeps, three-quarter-ton trucks and also two-and-a-half-ton trucks. After four weeks, Floyd decided to change his M.O.S.(Military Occupational Specialty) I wanted to continue to drive trucks, but Floyd became a clerk, so he went to clerical school. Since we both took typing in high school, Floyd was going to do well.

I loved driving a different vehicle weeks on end. I passed driving school, and after graduation, we stood in line for our orders. My orders were for Manheim, Germany. The majority of my classmates heard their names called for Southeast Asia—South Vietnam.

I shipped out to Brooklyn, New York, to wait for a ship to Bremerhaven, Germany. My eighteenth birthday happened around that time, and two days later I boarded a ship called the *Darby* for the nine-day crossing with my fellow two thousand shipmates. The first three days onboard were glorious. Then the seasickness started; I did not eat anything for the next five days, and I lost seventeen pounds in total. My weight was down to 114 when we arrived in the West German port of Bremerhaven on August 19, 1964.

A courier was there to meet soldiers going to different sectors in Germany, France, and Holland. My guide rode on the train with everyone going to Manheim. There were four large army bases in that area. From the station in Mannheim, I was dropped off on the front doorsteps of Taylor barracks, a three-story World War II German Army barracks. When I walked in I looked like a baby-faced ninety-pound weakling.

This was the 68th Transportation Company with sixty huge, old semis. Ninety-nine percent of the time I was on my own, taking trailers filled with all sorts of things for our troops in three different countries, from commissary goods to ammunition, from the US Army to the US Air Force. We also went to the borders of five other countries, some in Eastern Europe. I was barely eighteen, looking like fourteen; they must have thought twice before letting me take the wheel of an eighteen-wheeler. Thank God they did. I loved that job for thirty-two months and was a top miler with over one hundred thousand miles accrued by the end of my listing. Then I had to go to a transport school in the beginning of my German assignment to be taught German, French, and Dutch road signs plus map reading along with German language lessons, which were pretty basic. The training barracks in Mannheim were close to downtown, and I had to be driven by the commanding officer's jeep driver until my army driver's license for Europe was issued. Our group's huge flatbed trucks were stationed here; they were used to transport thirty-two-ton tanks, mostly used to go in convoy to Berlin through parts of Eastern Europe. After school, I was assigned to truck #23 over at Taylor barracks. It was fantastic to have my own truck after four weeks of schooling.

Floyd arrived two months later. He was stationed at Coleman Barracks with a fixed wing company as a clerk. He was confined to an office all day, quite different from my job out on the roads. We got together as often as we could.

Weekends were the times to hang out with my friends over at Taylor Barracks, and on one Saturday in the early afternoon Floyd was walking into the ground floor hallway and was attacked by my platoon sergeant, thinking it was me. We had an ongoing, good-natured "war" between the two of us. He did apologize when Floyd told him he was my twin brother, and we all had a good laugh.

Floyd was well liked by my fellow truck drivers and company clerks. However, four months later his company was moved outside of Stuttgart. Now he was over three hours away. I would stop by on my way to see him since his barracks were a few miles off the autobahn on the way to Munich, Garmisch-Partenkirchen, Dachau, or Augsburg, Floyd was getting depressed to the point where he had trouble with his throat. He ended up in Heidelberg Hospital. The army doctor could not diagnose what was causing the swelling; this was in May of 1965.

Floyd came to see me in Mannheim one weekend. He asked me to volunteer with him for Vietnam. We could go home for one month then serve thirteen months in that war zone. I told Floyd I loved my job, loved Germany, and loved traveling throughout Western Europe. It seemed my twin and I were starting to go our own separate ways. I was able to get a consignment to Munich that Sunday evening for the purpose of dropping Floyd off at his barracks, said good-bye, and went on my way hoping Floyd would stay safe.

Floyd was off to the US for the month of July and then to South Vietnam in August. He was put in a placement company. Floyd had to pull guard duty on the perimeter of his base, and it sounded pretty scary. He was put into a combat engineer unit, and we wrote to each other once a month.

Our brother Fred was also sent to Vietnam for four months with his unit being deployed out of Fort Sill. He was twenty-five years old when he was drafted, and everyone thought it was so cruel to be drafted so late. Fred was promoted to sergeant in just twenty months, after receiving a bronze star for bravery beyond the call of duty. Our family found out later how it happened: his unit was running out of ammunition and two different trucks were sent out for supplies never to return. Fred volunteered to try to get through and was successful, for which he was awarded the bronze medal.

Floyd wrote to say he'd tried to meet up with Fred in Saigon before Fred was to return back to the States. Then

Floyd was off to the States; he was able to get an early out. With his extra pay he bought a Camaro sports car. In Brandon, he met Marlene Bothwell; they fell in love and eloped early the following year, since she was sixteen years old. I was happy for them.

Floyd wrote to tell me that Fred stayed home inside his room for several months with post-traumatic stress symptoms; however, Floyd did persuade him one night to go out to the Whataburger drive-in where Fred once had a girlfriend waitressing. This was the start of Fred getting better and going back to the *Tampa Tribune*, where they held his job open.

**

While in Germany I started to mature. I was finally growing up. My work ethic improved and my attitude to my superiors became more respectful and courteous. This resulted in me achieving the rank of E5 in just over two years of service which is remarkable in peace time. Meanwhile, nineteen sixty-six came in quickly. We were all issued new International Harvester Cab-Over Tractors with ten forward gears. There was a ledge in the back long enough for my army blow-up mattress. I had to watch my speed in this one. It had a fiberglass body, much lighter than the WWII vintage tractors. I loved this truck much more than the last one.

A new driver arrived about this time, young and also from Florida. He was with us for a month of training, riding shotgun to learn the ropes. He came to me to ask if he could borrow my suit, as his wife was due to give birth the next day. Two weeks later, while he was riding shotgun with another driver and bobtailing (with no trailer behind the truck), they were hit by another truck and the rider's door was flung open, throwing him out and killing him. What a tragedy for his wife. I still think about him from time to time and wish I could remember his wife's name. My suit was returned, but I really would not have cared if he had been buried in it. I suppose his army dress suit was more appropriate.

I decided to go to Florida in June of 1966. I will always remember the cost of my airline ticket from Frankfurt to Tampa: $572.00 round trip—more than two months' pay. Mom was really glad to see me, and so was Dad—a nice shock. They could not do enough for me. Mike was doing all of the chores now. I borrowed Mom and Dad's car a lot and got a date with a girl named Alice out of Providence Baptist Church. I do not believe she was too impressed with me. But she was a beautiful, graceful, and had very good manners.

Mr. George who was from the church and headed the local Boy Scouts, asked me to help take the Boy Scout Troops on a camping trip to Gatlinburg, Tennessee. When we came home, there was a party at Larry Summerall's house. Franklin Griffiths was riding with me on the way home when we ran off the road into a tree. I spent three nights in Tampa General Hospital, and it delayed my trip back to Germany by fifteen days. Dad's car was totaled, but he never got upset. What a difference from when we left! How things could have been if he had been more tolerant during my early teenage years.

At the end of July, I was back in the barracks in Germany. I was visited by a reenlistment NCO from headquarters. He wanted to sign me up for a further six-year enlistment and promised me a $5200 bonus and helicopter flight training at Fort Rucker, Alabama. I very politely said, "No thanks."

In late December a friend of mine, Sam Castle, and his wife introduced me to Nikki, a beautiful twenty-year-old schoolteacher from Harrow on the Hill, London. She had a posh, "cotton in her mouth" accent, and I was struck through my heart. After dating Nikki for a week, I asked her to marry me. Nikki said yes, but I would have to meet her mom and dad.

The next week we were invited to a party in Heidelberg with Larry Cook and his German girlfriend. While in Heidelberg I took Nikki to the castle overlooking the river where there is fantastic cellar bar with large wine barrels. We flew to London the next week and met Jack and Flo, her parents, at Heathrow Airport. I was so nervous that I left Jack's duty-free Scotch and Flo's Harvey's Bristol Cream sherry in the parking garage against the wall. Jack was so disappointed.

I told Flo and Jack I was very much in love with their beautiful daughter and could not imagine going through life without her. After I asked Jack for Nikki's hand, Flo sat us down and said we could get married after a ten-month wait. This meant I had to come back to England after my army discharge.

Nikki invited most of her neighborhood friends over, including all the Claytons. I remember David Clayton's girlfriend, Jill, had this look as if to say, "Who is this American boy who wants to marry our Nikki?" Little did we know that we would all become friends forever. I fell in love with London and could not wait to get back to Taylor Barracks to put the paperwork in for the European discharge from the Army.

Chapter 5

Life with John

Although it was hard to top 1965, 1966 became my favorite year ever. John and I were engaged, he was finishing at the university, and we were making wedding plans. Daphne already had a young child, Lyn was going steady with Peter, and Nikki was dating John's friend from the university, Brian. Dave Clayton was dating Jill Charles, a grammar-school friend of Nikki's; Eddie Clayton was dating Lyn Tuffin; and Clive, my old boyfriend, was dating Tricia. Everyone was in love, it seemed!

I finished my three-year apprenticeship at last and couldn't wait to leave Francis and Elizabeth. My boss was a sour man, always stressed; who wouldn't be with girls like me to keep under control? I was ready for new experiences. As well as doing hair at home, I got a job at a local bakery. They ended up making our wedding cake for a very good price. John and I lived for our weekends and being together. There were still lots of parties and get-togethers. We went to the movies and met up with friends at the pub; it was a wonderful, carefree life. The worst thing that happened was running out of petrol in the middle of nowhere.

Boeing was recruiting graduates from London University to work on the new 747. At that time, I had a temporary job at Derry & Toms department store in

Kensington selling wigs. John came in one day and said, "Would you like to go to Seattle and live for at least one year?' I said yes right away without a second thought, and so we started making plans. We had to have medicals, and there were tons of forms to fill in plus a visit to the American Embassy. When we told Mum and Dad, Dad was delighted for us, but poor Mum was upset that John would be taking her only child away. Nevertheless, that was the way it was going to be.

Our wedding day was set for September 17, 1966. I got my dress and Nikki's, a deep pink with a matching little pillbox hat; she was going to be my bridesmaid. With everything organized, John and I went down to Weymouth and worked in a big, old hotel. John was a wine waiter and I was a chambermaid. One of my duties was to empty potties from under the bed—hard to believe now! The head housekeeper was very strict, and she inspected every corner of every bed. It was hard physical work, but we were free in the afternoons to go and enjoy the sea and the coffee bars. Of course, we slept in different annexes of the hotel, but we managed to get a lot of time together. I remember sneaking down to the kitchen at night and getting food to take back to the room. That's me, breaking the rules again!

The World Cup of soccer was on then, and Nikki and Brian came down to watch the final match together in the hotel lounge with lots of other guests and employees. When England won, the place exploded—I will never forget that joyous moment.

We came home to Little Chalfont the first week of September. One day, before the wedding, we went up to Carterton to visit John's parents, and John and his father decided to play some golf. I said I would go along. His dad took a swing, and the ball hit me right in the chest. It shook me up, but no real harm done. All I could think was, thank goodness it didn't hit me in the mouth or the eye, just days before the wedding.

The big day finally came, and it was sunny and warm. Nikki and I got our hair done at Francis and Elizabeth, and then we went home and got dressed. Mum gave us both a glass of wine, which not only relaxed us but also made us very giggly. I remember when it was time to go, I just stuck my headdress on, never even checking it in the mirror. It dawned on me when it was too late, but luckily it looked OK.

John and I were married in a lovely little church on the village green in Chenies, Buckinghamshire. It was a beautiful day, the happiest of my life, and I was sure John felt the same. I knew with absolute certainly that the promise I made that day I would keep my whole life. The reception was at the King's Head Hotel in Amersham, and even though my grandmother, Rose, would not come to the church because she was Christadelphian, she was at the reception and that made me very happy.

Between the wedding and leaving for Seattle in late November, John and I both got odd jobs so we'd have a little money to go with us. Mum and Dad let us stay with them for nothing, which helped out a lot, but it was a little tense with Mum. I worked as a lunchtime barmaid and waitress at a pub a few miles away in the heart of Buckinghamshire. It was a great job, and the couple that owned it was very nice. Lunchtimes were very busy so I made good tips and the time went quickly.

It was close to my last shift when, on the way home, probably going too fast down a narrow country lane, I crashed head-on into a garbage truck. My head hit the roof of the car—we didn't have seat belts in those days—but apart from that I was OK. The car unfortunately wasn't, so we left it there and the garbage men took me home in the truck. At this point, I think my dad gave up on the A35. I had intended that my mum should have it when we left so she could learn to drive. It was not meant to be, and Dad sold it for scrap.

**

In late November it was time to leave for Seattle. We had chosen to go on the *Queen Mary* to New York and then fly the rest of the way to Seattle. It was all paid for by Boeing, so we thought we'd make the most of it. The trip took six days; the cabin was pretty small but we enjoyed exploring the huge ship. Since it was November, the weather was cold, and they would bundle us up with a blanket on the deck chairs and bring us hot cups of Bovril. The food was amazing; we ate five times a day. Even though we were seasick the fourth day, we both still put on about five pounds.

Someone from Boeing picked us up at the Seattle airport and took us to a motel in Renton. Despite the fact it rained for seventeen straight days, we were excited at starting a new life. We found an apartment on East Olive Street and managed to scrape together enough money to buy a secondhand Mustang. This was fun; we were actually setting up house together. John started work and was given the task of designing a toilet seat for the aircraft—not quite what he expected.

I now had to get a job. My hairdressing qualifications were not recognized in America, but I finally got hired by a rather strange woman who had a small wig shop and styled and cleaned wigs for customers. There was one other girl working there, who was also a little odd, but I thought it was better than nothing for now. After a month, I went for an interview at the Seattle First National Bank and got the job of a trainee teller. I loved that job. Almost everything was done by people then, not computers. It was a challenge to balance each night, and if we were more than five dollars out, the Federal Bank Adjusters were called in and you could not go home until it was sorted out. Thankfully, it never happened to me. I could walk to work from the apartment, and the views of the mountains were breathtaking. At lunchtime, I'd go to the drugstore, sit down at the counter, and have a grilled cheese sandwich—so American.

John was definitely disillusioned with his job. I guess when you are young, you think that because you have a degree, you deserve a top job. But of course, you still have to climb the ladder starting at the bottom. Christmas was approaching, and we were going to be alone, or so we thought. Another young couple, John and Jean Hays, was managing the apartments we lived in and knew we were far from home. They asked us to join them for Christmas dinner. We have been friends ever since.

Meanwhile, Nikki had gone over to Germany with a group of English people to sell encyclopedias, and she met Lloyd Wiggins, a soldier from Florida. After returning home for Christmas, she went back to Germany, and within two weeks, Lloyd proposed. She had written to tell me all about this handsome soldier boy and sounded so happy and excited, every other boyfriend had disappeared off the radar. I wanted to be there with her, to share the joy, as she had been with me the year before. Trans-Adlantic phone calls were expensive back then so we only got to talk for a few minutes occasionally, but I could tell that this was the real thing and we could not wait to meet him!

In Seattle, John and I were certainly homesick at times, and John found his work boring; so we decided that after the year's contract was up, we'd go home. We started the ball rolling by packing stuff up and sending it surface mail. We thought we'd go by rail across Canada, and so we booked a train and the flight from Montreal to London.

But when we had just a few months left in Seattle, as it can so often happen in life, things started to change. John and Jean introduced us to other friends, and we went on hikes, explored the state, and started to enjoy our lives a lot. For our first anniversary, we went down to San Francisco with John and Jean, who was pregnant with their first child. It was very foggy when we got there, but we still enjoyed it, staying only one night because we all had to get back to work. We shared one big room, and John and Jean let us have the vibrating bed. They even put a quarter in for us!

By the time December came, we really regretted our decision to leave. John and Jean threw us a wonderful farewell dinner with a British theme, placemats in the shape of horse guards etc. It was very thoughtful, and we were sad to leave.

We arrived home in mid-December 1967. Nikki and Lloyd had married at St. Georges Church on October 7, 1967. We were so sorry to have missed the wedding, and we had not ever met Lloyd. But they were there to meet us at the airport along with both Mum and Dad and John's mother. It was back to Little Chalfont for a party. What a great homecoming it was, and all of our regrets disappeared.

We had a lot of fun over the Christmas holidays, catching up with friends, especially with Nikki and Lloyd. John and Lloyd immediately liked each other, which was great for Nikki and me. We went up to London to see the lights and have a pub meal. I was the designated driver, as one champagne was always my limit. I was not very used to driving in London, and we were soon going down a one-way street the wrong way! Luckily we got away unscathed. We were amazed how Lloyd adapted so well to the British way of life and the cold weather after living in Florida.

John and I found a bedsit in Wembly Park, a definite comedown from our Seattle apartment, and I got a job as an invoice clerk. It was the most boring job I ever had, sitting at a desk all day with a pile of invoices on the left side that had to be dealt with and end up on the right side—done! There was a big clock on the wall, which I checked about every five minutes; how could a day be so long? When John picked me up after work, I was so pleased to see him! He realized quickly that he wasn't really interested in aeronautics after all. Computers were the latest thing, and they really piqued his interest. Soon he got a job with a computer company and immediately felt that this was going to be his future.

We found a nice basement suite on Pinner Road, Harrow. A new singer called Elton John apparently lived down the road from us, and everyone was talking about him but we never got to see him. I found a new and much better job at the *Harrow Observer* newspaper as a receptionist/relief switchboard operator and classified ads clerk. I loved the hustle and bustle of a newspaper; there were two other girls in the front with me, and we had a great time. The switchboard was the old plug-in sort. I enjoyed working that; it was just like in the movies. My wages were ten pounds a week, and I thought that I was rich!

In February Lloyd was forced to leave the country due to immigration problems, and Nikki was getting ready to join him in Florida while living at home again. After all the paperwork was done, she was due to leave the beginning of April. John and I were going to miss them both very much.

Almost the entire group was married by now, so there were a few less parties, more dinners together, and we started playing bridge. I always thought that John was a lot more intelligent than me, but he never encouraged that idea. He told me that if I had taken all the steps that he had taken, I would be equally smart—I'm still not so sure about that! His brother Peter was brilliant; he had a degree from Oxford, and when we played bridge, he would know every card in my hand. It blew my mind then; now, however, I know how it's done.

For our second anniversary, we went down to Bude Devon with Daphne and Alan and three-year-old Steven. We rented a cottage and celebrated our two very good years. About this time, John and I started talking about having children, visualizing what they would look like and how many we would like to have. We believed, like a lot of people, that a boy and a girl would be ideal.

In winter of 1968, I stopped taking the birth control pill but my cycle was messed up. I waited a few more months then decided to see my doctor. He sent me to the University College Hospital in London, which was a teaching hospital. I don't ever remember talking to a doctor there, just lying on the examination table with about a dozen students standing there with the doctor talking to them. The second visit he gave me an injection and sent me home.

A number of weeks later, John and I were on a weekend trip when I started bleeding. He rushed me to the hospital, and it turned out to be a threatened miscarriage. They put in an IV, and I was put on total bed rest. It was the end of my job at the newspaper and the beginning of almost seven months in the hospital. We were not really ready to start a family at that point, as we were living in a very small basement suite with not much money. I just wanted to be healthy and ready to conceive. I felt that I had never gotten the chance to talk about our situation, and I was certainly not given any information about the chances of a multiple birth. Rules at the hospital were tightened up quite a bit after my experience. Couples would have it clearly explained to them about what could occur if given fertility drugs.

At two months, they told us we were expecting twins. At four months they upped it to triplets, the next month it became five, and by the sixth month it was seven! I was allowed to go home for the odd weekend, and I looked like I was ready to give birth even at only four months. I had to be very careful, but I did enjoy those couple of days away from the hospital. John was wonderful to me during that time, and I felt very special. Back at the hospital I was given my own room, and I could have whatever I wanted to eat as long as it included six eggs a day in some form. I remember craving smoked salmon and frozen Victoria sponges.

Poor John, during this time he was going to work and spending every spare minute visiting me. I was very emotional when it came time for him to leave; I just cried and cried. Peter, my brother-in-law, was a constant visitor with his girlfriend. They were each allowed to smoke in the room, and the doctor even encouraged me to have a glass of sherry every day! How times have changed. My younger brother-in-law, Geoff, was still living in Carterton, so he only came up to London occasionally. I always appreciated the friends and family that visited me during those long months.

One day a week, I had to starve for ten hours for a test that was being done for research purposes. They were the longest days, but I was getting such great care that I couldn't really complain. A few times during those months, I had contractions. and I was quickly put on a drip to stop them. Word was getting out now about the multiple birth, and one day a newspaper man burst into my room and took my picture. I was a little disturbed by that!

We hadn't actually told my Mum and Dad about the latest number, but one morning on the radio they announced that Rosemary Letts was expecting seven babies. I called John, and he immediately contacted my parents. It was big news now, and I started getting tons of mail from all over the world. A lot was good, but there was also quite a lot that was hateful. My darling John shielded me from the latter. Meantime, our doctor, Mr. Brandt, had put John in contact with a marketing man, Andrew Miller. He was going to look into making some money for us, but there needed to be seven babies. Each number less would be that much less money. It seemed awfully mercenary, and I wasn't comfortable with it. He told me that in the future all I would be doing was living on a desert island writing a book about my life with John and the babies.

Chapter 6

My European Army Discharge

Lloyd's Story

I arrived back in London after being away for ten days and went to see the old man's clerk, Radomski, the next morning. He worked on it all day and told me that evening at the club that I did not have enough time for the paperwork to go through. I would have to extend for one month. I said to him, "Do it in the morning," and he replied, "You really are head over heels in love with Nikki and London." I couldn't wait to see them both again.

The next four months went by so slowly. Nikki would try to call often, but being in a barracks and on the road all the time, I was difficult to get hold of. It was easier for me to stop when I was on the road at a German phone exchange and call her. It was expensive but well worth it.

I finally got my discharge papers on March 27, 1967, and called Nikki to tell her I would be arriving on April 2. The day of my departure from the army in Europe, I flew into London that very night. I could not believe all of the lights. The streets were lit up in the suburbs like it was daylight; all the lights were yellow. It was an awesome sight!

The plane landed at Heathrow airport and I went through immigration. The officer asked me what the purpose of my trip to England was and also how long my stay was going to be. I showed him my army papers and told him I was with the US government and that my stay was going to be indefinite. He let me through. Nikki and her parents were there to meet me. Jack made sure I did not lose the duty-free liquor this time! What a wonderful feeling, being free from the US Army and with my future wife.

I called Mom the next day and told her my plan was to get married in six months, and then be home within twelve months. The army would fly for free anyone getting a European discharge to Maguire Air Force Base where all the paperwork would be finalized. My mom said, "Boy, maybe you should get home now." I repeated my plans to have Nikki for my wife.

I got a job the next week at the Ruislip Air Force Base commissary and found a bedsit in South Harrow, just a bedroom with a bathroom. It was not a comfortable place to stay on any evening, but Nikki would walk over or I would walk to her house. The hassle was worth it all when we were together. Every weekend, we were at someone's house for a party, including the engagement party that Flo and Jack, Nikki's parents, threw for us. Before that, we had to pick out rings. We walked to Harrow on the Hill my second Saturday in London. Nikki liked a large ruby cluster gold ring. It was beautiful! I still remember the cost was thirty-two pounds, about eighty-four dollars; this was equal to three weeks' work at the commissary.

I met Nikki's extended family, friends, and neighbors the next weekend at Nikki's house. Dave Williamson, one of Nikki's old boyfriends, was there. He was a very nice young man, very tall and the manager of an electronics store on the High Street in Harrow. Vera (Duck) lived next door. We called her Duck because, being a Londoner, she would respond to everyone young by saying, "Yes, me duck." I also met Lynda and Peter Garwood. Lynda was slender, beautiful, and very witty. She worked for an assurance company in Harrow on the Hill. We would often meet Lynda for a pub lunch a few steps away from her office. I don't want to leave out any of Nikki's friends because it shows just how magnetic she was! Wherever we landed either on vacation or setting up house, we became accepted as friends instantly. Her educated, very British accent was always a showstopper.

The Tobiases were a very nice family who lived next door. Their house was part of Nikki's parents' semi-detached house. They were Allan and Shirley, and their son, Peter, had passion growing up to play cricket. Nikki and I were to see Peter again later in life at a sixtieth party for all of us.

There were so many people at this party. I met Ro's parents, David and Vera Egerton (I hadn't met Ro yet but I had heard all about her friendship with Nikki), and Ro and Nikki's childhood friend, Jacque Bell, and her boyfriend, David Bevan, a rugby player and the epitome of an English gentleman. I felt that Nikki's aunts, Rose and Gert and Philly Pott, were watching to see what kind of "bloke" Nikki was going to marry. Thank goodness we looked happy together— not only looked it but felt it, and it showed.

The next two months went by quickly. We spent weekends playing cards with friends for pennies—these pennies were huge, the size of silver dollars! We played with David and Vera, Ro's parents, either in Harrow or Rickmansworth. Ro was in Seattle, Washington, with her husband John for a year. This was in 1966 when they took the *Queen Mary* over to America.

On one of our visits to David and Vera's, Ro's dad wanted to know if I would be interested in working for a new company in the county of Buckinghamshire. The company was called Agriculture Business Consultants, and they advised farmers and contractors on how to repair the ground when the pipelines were laid. The North Sea oil and natural gas find was a bonanza for England, which was in dire straits until these finds. The owner of ABC, Jim Fellow Smith, was a very large, energetic man. He had two partners, an Aussie and a Kiwi, who worked in the field. Their headquarters were in an old, stately manor house in the country.

David drove me there for an interview. They asked me what qualifications I had to advise various parties. I told Jim that, being brought up on a farm in rural Florida, we planted grasses with all of their preparations, and I had three years of schooling with the Future Farmers of America. He said, "You're hired." I told Jim Fellow Smith that I would like to give my boss in Ruislip two weeks notice. He said that was fine, and he would see me in two weeks.

I had my last party that weekend with Nikki and friends, and I knew it was going to be nose to the grindstone. We never talked wages until that Monday. I signed a contract as a consultant for seventy-five pounds a month, and I was responsible for paying taxes on that amount. We all were put up in the old stables converted to living quarters on the grounds of Shallstone Manor, halfway between Brackley and Buckingham.

There were a few Englishmen working with us. A great bunch of guys! Most lunchtimes we would pile into the company station wagon and go find a local pub that served food. There was this older, tall, heavyset Englishman with a drooping mustache. He would always order a pint of dark beer, and his mustache would be covered with froth. You could see his enjoyment with that first gulp!

We were now into September with one month to go until the wedding day. Odd weekends I would go see Nikki. One such weekend, I had to leave at four a.m. on Monday to catch trains to Tunbridge Wells to meet the crew at an inn for the week. The next morning we all ordered breakfast; when I ordered a T-bone steak and eggs, the Aussie and the Kiwi changed their orders. They said they wanted to eat steak for breakfast at least once.

The next weekend we were in Oxfordshire where the Thames River bank came close to the pipeline. It was warm that day. I had swum in the Alafia and Rheine Rivers, and I wanted to add the Thames to my repertoire. We stripped off to swim. These guys were also country boys; around our digs they all went barefoot. I hadn't seen guys like that since my childhood when we went everywhere barefooted except to church and school.

I left Shallstone Manor on October 5 and was dropped off at the bus stop to make my way to London. Two more days and I would be married. I wouldn't have blamed Nikki for not going through with it since my future prospects for a high-paying job in Britain or America were slim. Since I was working in Buckinghamshire and Nikki was teaching school in Harrow, we were apart a lot. Maybe that is why we enjoyed our time together so much, even having coffee in the Wimpy bar(a chain of hamburger restaurants) on Harrow High Street.

I got to Harrow on Thursday in time to meet Nikki coming out of school. We went for a drink at the Goodwill Pub and talked about where to go for our honeymoon. We wanted Pete Garwood as my best man. I stayed with Pete's mom and dad, Wyn and Archie, the night before our wedding. I was very fond of them.

The wedding day, October 7, 1967, finally was here. I went to the church with Pete, a little nervous but not much.

Pete and I were standing at the front of the church waiting, it seemed like, for hours. He would talk, I guess to keep me from becoming too nervous, and then all of a sudden, the music "Here Comes the Bride" started. I turned around to see Jack escorting his beautiful young daughter down the aisle. I felt like smiling and crying at the same time, if that was even possible. Jack handed Nikki over to me, and we gazed at each other so lovingly the vicar had to clear his throat to get our attention so we could say our vows. When Nikki said, "I do," my dream actually came true. Her vows and my dream lasted a lifetime. We kissed quickly to seal it all, then off to the vestibule to sign the papers. Lynda Garwood was Nikki's bridesmaid, and she also looked stunning. Unfortunately Ro and John were still in Seattle. Nikki's aunt Alma (Jack's sister and Nikki's middle name) and her husband, Eric, were my stand-in parents along with Lynda and Pete as witnesses on the wedding documents. I thanked them during my speech at the reception where we had a sit-down, proper meal.

Flo and Jack did us proud with such a grand wedding, dinner, dancing, and speeches from Jack, Pete, and me. I was so nervous that my Southern accent was hard to understand, so Nikki assured me that no one would notice if I did mess it up. We were off to Wales the next day on our honeymoon, then on to Swindon on the way back to Harrow. We also stopped by to see Pete and Lynda in High Wycombe.

We moved to Shallstone Manor and set up house in the old laundry converted into a two-bedroom house upstairs. Downstairs were a garage and storage. I went back to work with the boys, and Nikki interviewed for a teaching job at the elementary school in Buckingham. She started two weeks later when the teacher she replaced went on maternity leave.

The London gang came over to Shallstone for a Guy Fawkes party in November. Guy Fawkes was executed for the attempted blowing up of Parliament in London in the early sixteen hundreds. We had a large bonfire and plenty of food, hot cider, and bitters. Some of the gang stayed over, sleeping wherever they found a place on the floor. Waking up the next morning, I could not see out the window and jumped out of bed to find that there was a half inch of ice on the inside window pane. I was used to winters being a little warmer, so I got back in bed quickly to tell Nikki. She replied that I would have to get used to it because winter was just starting and this old place was not insulated.

Nikki and I went to London on Friday, November 17, for Jacque Bell and David Bevan's wedding in St. Albans at the cathedral. Nikki's father, Jack, and Jacque's father, also Jack, partied, mostly at the bar, all night. Then Nikki's father drove us to Shallstone that night. I tried to get him to let me drive, but he said he was OK. It was a miracle we made it! Clara, my guardian angel and now also Nikki's, must have been looking out after us. Well, we made it somehow.

Nikki and I traveled back to London in December to meet Ro and John coming in from the states. I liked them both right away. We were invited to Ro's parents' house in Rickmansworth for the homecoming party. Ro, John, Nikki, and I got together a few days later because we all wanted to see the Christmas lights in Oxford Circus and Trafalgar Square. We had a pub meal then went back to Harrow. Ro had only one champagne, as she was the designated driver. We still managed to drive the wrong way on a one-way street in the middle of London, but we made it back to Flo and Jack's house safely. We did tease Ro unmercifully and often for her driving in London.

January came in with a New Year's party for all the friends. Not long after that, I asked Nikki to take my passport to the home office in London to get me a visa for the purpose of staying in England indefinitely. I traveled back to Shallstone because of work. Nikki still had a few more days off from teaching during the school holiday. Unbeknown to me, Nikki lost my passport close to the Holborn police station. She never told me, and I did not think about asking her, since I was busy and working out of town most days.

British immigration and tax authorities tracked me down. They took all of the money out of my bank account and gave me thirty days to leave the country. I thought that was nice since I had told them an untruth at immigration several months ago. This was the beginning of February. I got my official letter to check in with immigration when I left, and I had to be gone by March 14, 1968. Before leaving we visited the aunties, cousins, plus lots of friends—Nikki received a call from Auntie Rose for us to go for a lunch in London. We met Rose for a lovely meal where she talked about her son, Nikki's cousin David Squires; little did we know we would socialize with David and his wife Sarah in the future. When we asked for the tab, Auntie Sis stepped in with her loving way to say it was her treat. We were a little short of funds by this time.

We contacted the US Air Force to set up a departure date from Mildenhall, England. I was going to Maguire Air Force Base in the US. They also said that since I was an E5 (rank) and married, they would ship a crate from Shallstone to Tampa, up to two thousand pounds. This was a nice surprise, for we were getting lots of wedding presents for our new home, and the Danby china and Wedgewood were heavy. There was enough money to fly Nikki to Tampa and also to get me by bus to Ocala from Maguire Air Force Base. Floyd went down to the Greyhound terminal to pay the extra six dollars to Tampa. Moving was a pretty daunting task for us.

Nikki's paperwork was going to take another four weeks with the US Embassy in London. After interviews, physicals, and also a blood test, she was going to be able to join me within a month after my departure. The week I left, Nikki moved back in with her parents, but the night before my flight we went to stay with Philly, Bert and the boys since they lived close to Mildenhall, the air base. I did not want to go; it would have been easier to live in England for a time. But when I arrived at Maguire Air Force Base, it did feel good to be on American soil again.

**

The bus trip to Tampa was so tiring—over forty-eight hours and no money for food, just coffee. I made a promise to never go by bus again. The bus trip was also emotional with the emptiness of not having Nikki with me. It was so hard to sleep on the plane and the bus that it exacerbated my loneliness. I hated not knowing what Nikki was going through. She was not only my wife, she was my life. I knew that whatever I did in the future, it would be for her.

Floyd picked me up on the evening of March 21, 1968. Since I now had an English accent, he asked me not to talk so loud because everyone would think I was gay—how things have changed!

I got a job with R&R Supply Company in Tampa. It was a difficult place to work; I don't believe they liked ex-military people. I started out at $1.50 per hour and worked sixty-plus hours a week for seven months. The people there were horrible in their attitude and work ethic. However, it was better than taking unemployment checks for weeks, which I first thought might be a good idea. But signing up for these benefits was not me; I realized that after standing in line for a period of time. This seemed wrong since there were plenty of jobs to be had, especially in the Tampa area.

My parents attitude toward me was surprisingly better than it had been four years before. Nikki would called often when I was not around, but the only person she could understand was Prissy; likewise they found her accent a little hard to understand. Nikki said to me one day that my parent's accents reminded her of a cartoon in England of Ma and Pa Bear of the Hillbilly Bears; of course, I never mentioned this to them.

Nikki finally arrived in late April. Mom and Dad threw us a party the night Nikki arrived in Tampa. They were all taken back by her beauty and personable demeanor. We lived with Prissy and her husband, Jerry, for three months. They had two beautiful, well-mannered children, Kathy and Phillip. Both kids were good at their studies, and Nikki and I hardly ever noticed them because they were extremely quiet. Prissy and Jerry wouldn't let us pay for anything so we saved five hundred dollars to put down on a house in Riverview. Nikki got a job as a teacher with the Maddox Private School.

In May, I put in my application with Delta Airlines hoping to find a way for Nikki to go home anytime she wanted. Uncle Wesley worked for National Airlines at the Tampa Airport. He and Aunt Gertha befriended us, and Gertha became Nikki's surrogate mother I believe, along with Prissy.

I kept calling Delta in Tampa, but the assistant station manager, Herb Neighbors avoided most or all of my calls.

Finally I'd had enough of calling, and Nikki and I went to Miami for interviews with Eastern, National, and Delta airlines. This was the weekend of our first wedding anniversary. Delta asked me to take their exam, and we waited in the office until the exam was marked. Then Delta's station manager asked us into his office. He wanted to know when I could start to work. I almost cried; we were both choked up so much. I asked him to please give me a week to let him know. I didn't tell him that we did not like Miami, but we both told him Tampa was our home and we would like to live there. He was very understanding.

Back at work at R&R Supply the following Tuesday, I took off early so I could catch Mr. Neighbors at the Tampa airport. I was lucky he would be able to see me, and I told him that Delta in Miami wanted to hire me. He asked me to also take the test, and after completing the test and having it graded, he said I would be contacted. I told him we had to let Miami know within the week. Delta called me and asked me to go to Atlanta that Friday for an interview. So on Thursday afternoon, I asked the manager at R&R Supply for another personal day off without pay. Delta flew me first-class to Atlanta early Friday morning, and the interview went well. I told the interviewer how much a job with Delta would mean to my wife and me.

The following Monday morning, Mr. Neighbors called me at work to tell me that I could start with Delta at Tampa Airport in two weeks. I said that sounded good because I could give R&R Supply two weeks' notice. But my manager said that if I did not need R&R Supply after two weeks, he would get a new employee in the next morning and I was to train him for four days and then leave. I told him, "If you don't need me for the next two weeks, you can't have me for the next four days." So I walked out the door without ever looking back. Somehow it was so wonderful to be able to walk away from a job that gave me not one ounce of pleasure.

I could not wait to get home to tell Nikki. On the way back to Riverview, I stopped at the Kash'n'Karry distribution warehouse in Ybor City, Tampa, where my brother-in-law worked as a butcher; this was Elaine's husband, Bud. I told him what had just happened, and he called the manager to ask if they needed any help for a couple of weeks. He said I could start the next morning stocking shelves at seven a.m. and the pay would be $1.50 an hour for a forty-hour week. I said, "Thank you, sir, for hiring me."

Nikki arrived home from Maddox Private School at approximately four thirty p.m. She was so excited when I told her about my Delta that she called her mother and woke her up in Harrow, London, to tell her the wonderful news. Hooray! Even after all these years later, it still feels wonderful.

Chapter 7

The Birth

Ro's Story

When I was about seven months pregnant, I started having severe contractions. Instead of calling for the nurse, for some reason I responded to my instincts and kept quiet. But the pain was worsening, and when my doctor dropped in to see me, he went straight into action. The babies were born a few hours later by C-section. In less than three minutes there were six babies; one girl was stillborn, and as it turned out the seventh was a shadow on the ultrasound. There were two placentas with three children in each one. I was told later that if they had been born any later, I would have lost another one. That would have been Gary, my only boy. My first words coming around were, "Where are the other two?"

They had all been taken down the elevator to be put in incubators right away, and I was told that there was only a fifty-fifty chance of their surviving. However, I knew different—there was absolutely no doubt in my mind that they would all survive. The next morning the birth was headline news in most London newspapers and across Europe. Now Andrew, the marketing man had to rethink the situation. He'd said that if only three survived we'd be out on our own. If that were the case, we planned to move to Chester where property was reasonable. John started looking into buying a house there; he was evidently not so sure about them making it. He told me later how worried he was about us all.

Now, the press was in full force. Everyone wanted an exclusive. We chose the *Daily Mirror* because they only wanted a one-year contract, and we did not want our children exposed to too much publicity, especially as they grew older. We certainly needed the money, first and foremost to buy a house. Our small one-bed basement suite would not do any longer. John was so good; he held it all together and made all the decisions. I was still in La-La Land! We got to see the babies pretty soon after the birth, but of course we couldn't touch them, just look in amazement at their size. Cara was the biggest at two pounds, thirteen ounces, down to Gary at one pound, twelve ounces; yet they were all perfect.

There were lots of picture taking and stories in magazines all over the world. Andrew, our marketing man, got the BBC interested, and we started negotiations with them for a documentary. The babies were the focus now—I was old news! A few days later I was released from the hospital, and John picked me up. I was still quite weak and had no clothes I could fit into, so John said, "Let's go shopping on Oxford Street and you can buy anything you like; don't even look at the price tag."

I lasted barely ten minutes before I got a very severe pain in my chest. John called for an ambulance, and before I knew it I was back in the hospital. This time I was put in a general ward along with thirty other patients with pneumonia, which was exactly what I had—in both lungs.

The nurse came in with a large needle, which she plunged into my backside. Shortly afterward the pain subsided. I was then sat upright with a spittoon and told to cough as much as I could. Next to me was a woman crying all the time and calling out for "John" (who never came)— all through the night. In the morning they drew the curtains around her bed. She had died that night and they took her away. So I spent my first Christmas after the kids were born back in the hospital and was not even allowed to see them. John visited as much as he could manage running between the babies and me. We had so looked forward to a Christmas at home, but it was not meant to be.

Now, one would think that this would be a good time to quit smoking, but the first thing I wanted after leaving the hospital was a cigarette. Most everyone I knew smoked; including Nikki who always loved her cigarettes and never wanted to quit we just did not think of the consequences or risk to our health. It would take me another sixteen years to finally break the habit!

The quintuplets made remarkable progress. Soon John and I were able to hold them and feed them; it was an incredible experience. They were so tiny but amazingly tough.

Some money had come through from the *Daily Mirror* so we rented a small flat in Regents Park, not too far from the hospital. It was a beautiful area of London where we would be able to walk the babies. Baby number one, whom we named Cara Dawn, and baby two, Sharon Marie, were heavier than the other three and got to the five-pound mark pretty quickly, so we could take them home to the flat. Photographers were there to record the occasion. It was our first taste of parenthood! One time I actually got asked for my autograph—I was dumbfounded! We'd had several names for boys ready—believing there would be more boys than girls for some unknown reason—so Gary John was decided on. I then picked Joanne and Tanya, and John came up with their second names, Nadine and Odele. I think Tanya forgave us.

Now we had to move quickly. The other three would be coming home in a few weeks and we had no home for them to come to. Money from the *Daily Mirror* and the BBC enabled us to get a house; we were grateful for that. We got absolutely nothing from the British government. Cow & Gate did provide us with milk for a year, which was a big help. John and I settled on a house in Dove Park Chorleywood that was fairly close to my parents and friends and also not too far from London.

Most importantly we could move in quite quickly. By the end of February we were all together at home and started to interview for help. We soon had two young, newly qualified nannies working for us. One girl was live-in, and the other was casual help. I found it a little difficult to share my house and my babies with virtual strangers, but I needed the help so I had to deal with it. We had a very organized routine, which I probably have to thank the girls for, and we had to be ready for either the newspaper to come, or more regularly, the BBC with a full crew for the whole day. There was always an interview segment, and sometimes it was a huge effort to talk on camera. There were a lot of crying babies in those early days. It seemed that at least one was always crying; it was very hard to have them all settled down at once. When that happened I would rush to the bed for a nap. I remember how wonderful that felt!

We had a double and a triple pushchair, and we always got quite a bit of attention when we were out for a walk. My mum and dad lived only a few miles away and helped whenever they could. They adored the babies but were a little overwhelmed, I think. John's mum, Doris Letts, was very supportive, too. She lived quite a bit farther away in Oxfordshire, and she was a wonderful knitter. For many years she provided sweaters, dresses, and cardigans for the children.

We got a yellow Volkswagen mini-bus, and I really enjoyed strapping them in their car seats and taking the five toddlers to Chorleywood Common for playtime. Sometimes John and I would take family trips farther afield; the kids loved going in the bus, and we had a lot of fun. I remember, though, it took a lot of patience getting all of them ready!

John now put his mind to supporting us all. He'd left his job when the babies were born, to get us set up in a home and organized, which took a few months. He thought starting his own business might be the answer and came up with the idea of placing students in jobs during summer holidays, so he created "Holiday Jobs." He got a small office over a fish-and-chips shop on Gouge Street, London. I was pretty busy at home so I wasn't involved in the new business, but I knew John was a very smart man and always supported his decisions.

The time came for the christening, early in September 1971. Nikki and Lloyd were Gary's godparents, but because Nikki was having a difficult pregnancy, they could not fly over from Florida. We had it at the same church we were married in, in Chenies Village, Buckinghamshire. Daphne and Alan Dempster, Pauline and Cris Porter, Lyn and Pete Garwood, and Liz and Tony Enfield were the other godparents. It was a beautiful September day, and of course the BBC was there to film it. The noise was deafening! All five of the babies cried the whole time, but the vicar stayed calm and we all put on brave faces.

Holiday Jobs only lasted a season, I'm not sure why it didn't fly, but I'm sure John took some valuable lessons from the experience. Through all of this, we both realized that we needed some time off to stay sane. John had a golf day and I had a "shopping" day. We so looked forward to them! And we were very thankful that we had such a great support team. We even took it one step further and decided to take a two-week holiday. I think I must have been showing signs of a breakdown. I do remember just wanting a "normal" life again, realizing that was not possible and just wanting to scream at the top of my voice—but stopping myself from doing it.

We thought what fun it would be to fly to New York and drive down to Florida and surprise Nikki and Lloyd. It was a fantastic trip, exactly what we needed. We saw Niagara Falls, the White House, and the Lincoln Memorial. It was January 1971, so we started in the snow and headed south through the Carolinas, the Blue Ridge Mountains, and Georgia; finally we were in the warm sunshine of Florida. We did surprise them for sure! It was so good to all be together again. Nikki was eight months pregnant and doing well now, and they took us to Lloyd's parents' home in Riverview. We had some real Southern cooking, picked grapefruit, and saw snakes and alligators. John and Lloyd played golf at a course next to Tampa Airport where John saw an alligator swimming in one of the ponds. This experience would entertain guests at dinner parties or barbecues for years. That trip really energized us, and we came home feeling much better. I felt I had gotten control of my life again.

We let the two young nannies go and employed a wonderful local girl called Anne, who was closer to my age and who was a very warm, loving, and down-to-earth person. We immediately got on, and I felt much more comfortable with her around. She was a great cook, and the kids loved the food she made; and she lived close by so there was no need to live-in. It all worked out much better.

Anne was dating Roger, a lovely, red-haired, young mechanic who had his own garage, and they were very happy. Today they are still happily married, still living in Chorleywood, and have two sons and several grandchildren.

We were no longer hounded by newspapers, but the BBC was still in the process of making the documentary. They came for one day every two weeks. It was always a very long day, but for the most part, the crew and director were very considerate, and we had a nice doctor of psychiatry interviewing us. He even invited us to his one-hundred-year-old cottage in the country. One day he attempted to hypnotize me, but I subconsciously resisted and it didn't work.

The money started to run out, and John told me we would have to sell the house and move somewhere a lot cheaper. I always trusted him implicitly so we started looking at places and planning what to do next. As there were no computers then, you had to go physically to look at property, so John took off and I went with him whenever I could. In the end we decided on Nupend Lodge in Longhope, Gloucestershire. It was quite a big, old, rundown house on an acre of land. There had been an elderly widow living in it by herself, and it was very dirty. I'll always remember the pantry with big meat hooks hanging from the ceiling and a marble slab. The shelves were thick with dead flies. We bought it for twelve thousand pounds.

Nikki and Lloyd came over from Florida with their new baby girl, Julliet, and we left all of our children with the grandparents and Anne and took them to see our new home-to-be. John had a real vision of what it could become, but that day, I had serious second thoughts as to whether we could cope with all of the work—and it was so far away from friends and family. Nikki was always so positive and encouraging, and she was sure we could do it. The men played golf, and the girls had a lovely day at Ross on Wye. It is a beautiful part of England. Before they left, we were delighted to be asked to be Julliet's godparents.

Chapter 8

The Delta Family

Lloyd's Story

I finally started at Delta—it was so great! I was going to do whatever it took to keep this job for Nikki so that she would be able to travel on a pass to her beloved Harrow any time she wanted. On the job I called everyone *sir*; I did not want to mess this job up in any way. There are times when you make decisions that are life-changing. My salary more than doubled with Delta Airlines, and Nikki and I knew that life was going to be different.

The next week I went to Miami for training for a week. In another week, fourteen new people were hired, and I had seniority on them. We were all put on six months probation. I met with the new guys, including Lee Anderson, who was married to Jimetta. Nikki I developed a friendship with them that was going to become lifelong. After my probationary period, Nikki went home on a Pan Am pass in June. It was the only way we could have afforded her ticket, which was 10 percent of the lowest applicable fare.

In September, Nikki and I, along with Lee and Jimetta Anderson, went to London. We had a great party with all of our friends. What a treat to have a way of traveling that would not have been possible without being an airline employee.

The next two years, without children for any of us, we traveled with the Andersons to London for the odd weekend party, to the Caribbean for holidays, to Vegas, New York, and San Francisco. It seemed that anytime we had off we were going on a plane somewhere. Pat and Judy Paleveda were also our traveling companions. Pat's dad and mom were a lovely, loving couple, and it was a pleasure being with them at their house and visiting them on Indian Rocks Beach. Pat and Judy and their family then moved to Atlanta, where Pat was transferred to Delta flight control. We would often fly up to Atlanta with the children to go to the Atlanta Braves baseball games. Back then tickets were a dollar each, and Judy would pack a picnic for all of us.

Nikki loved living the Florida life, with the airline life as an added bonus. But since we had a "peeping Tom" in Riverview, she wanted to move. So we sold our house in 1970 and bought one on Leone Avenue in South Tampa. This was a very, very good move. After moving to Tampa, our social life within the Delta airlines employees was busy. I started on the company fast-pitch softball team that was to last throughout my twelve-plus years at Delta.

In the summer of 1970, on a seven a.m. Saturday shift, Jim and I were working a DC8 turnaround to Atlanta. There was a jet brake waiting on the ground to be loaded onto a conveyor belt mounted on a truck. We had to lift this three-hundred-pound box three feet so we could put it in bin number one. The door was six feet off the ground, and as we picked it up I felt a pull in my lower stomach. I did not think anything of it, but by Monday it was starting to ache.

I went to see Dr. Zipser, a good friend. He examined me and diagnosed a hernia. As a child and teenager, I'd had two hernia operations done at the Plant City Baptist Hospital; working on the farm back then took its toll.

The next morning I went to see Joe Pavco, the assistant station manager. I told him what had happened, and he said that since the injury was not written up when it happened, Delta was not going to take responsibility for it. It is safe to say that Pavco did Delta no favors. After checking out my accident insurance, however, I discovered I would be compensated for the time out of work at 80 percent of my salary, tax free, with all surgeries taken care of as well.

I walked into Les Zipser's office that late afternoon with my Delta uniform on and told him about the Pavco episode. Les said, "Don't worry, Lloyd; you may need extra time to heal, say about six months."

I said, "I don't know, Les, Delta may not adhere to it." Les told me he would put it in a letter in a way that Delta would gladly give me six months' leave. The operation was OK, but the recovering was getting on Nikki's nerves. I was still bent over after a week, and one day I hobbled to the kitchen passing the TV on the way. I teasingly turned off the soap opera she was watching and told her to fetch my lunch. She went ballistic! She tried to kick me, and I said, "Not in the stomach!" That was a close shave.

Weeks later we both were getting cabin fever so Nikki said, "Let's go on that motoring trip we've been thinking about." She had been wanting to see Alabama, Georgia, and Louisiana. I said, "Great! Let's go to Alabama to see my cousins, my dad's kinfolk in Opp." The first night we stayed at a hotel in North Florida on the Georgia state line. We stopped in time for our five o'clock drinks, but it was a "dry" county—Nikki could not believe that—so we had a Coke. The next day we traveled on toward Opp. We stopped in an antique shop halfway there and this young girl was listening to Nikki's accent. She said, "Golly, y'all look just like us." She had never seen an English person before.

After a long day driving, we finally got to Andalusia, Alabama—very close to Opp—to stop at a store since Opp had no stores. We pulled into a Piggly Wiggly grocery store, and Nikki went in and left me to rest in the car. After about thirty minutes, I went inside to see where she was. She was surrounded by three large and wide black ladies, and I heard one say, "Now, missy say it real slow what you are looking for."

Nikki said really slowly, "So-da water." Everyone was staring at her.

I walked up and said, "She wants some seltzer."

They all said in unison, "Why, honey, why on earth didn't you tell us at the beginning that was what you wanted?"

When Nikki got back in the car, she did a big sigh and said, "How come they couldn't understand English?" I told her she needed an interpreter while in Alabama.

We pulled up to Uncle J.D. and Aunt May's house about six p.m. J.D. came out to the front porch, and his overall leggings came halfway down to his knees. He was also holding a fiddle. Nikki whispered, "I thought those people were only in the movies." After hugs and kisses, Aunt May called most of our cousins to come over, and she cooked chicken, dumplings, greens, and corn bread. Nikki ate very little; she did not like her food swimming in brine.

After the meal, J.D. said to us, "Your bed is made when you want to go to sleep." Nikki blurted out that we were already booked into a Holiday Inn. J.D. burst out with a big laugh and said, "Honey, closest Holiday Inn was across the Louisiana line more than two hours away." Then he said to me, "Your li'l wife sure has a sense of humor."

I replied, "Nikki is very humorous after a few drinks of homemade whiskey." J.D. howled.

After a huge breakfast of grits, homemade biscuits, and sausage with eggs, we were on our way. Nikki made sure there were no more cousins to visit. We headed back to Florida three weeks later and arrived back in Tampa to rest up after our trip. We sure did laugh a lot! We spent a lot of evenings at Floyd and Marlene's house in Pinecrest, barbecuing and having fun around the bonfire. Back in Tampa we played a lot of bridge with our Delta friends Lee and Jimetta Anderson at both of our homes, before and after dinner. There were always other Delta people stopping by, like Ed and Phyllis and Dale and Mary. These evenings lasted till midnight regardless of whether we all had to be at work by seven a.m. We also met lots of new friends outside of the Delta family in South Tampa through St. Mary's Episcopal Church.

After six months away from Delta, Pavco's secretary called me to set up a time to meet with the assistant station manager. I went to see him the next morning. Mr. Pavco said I had been out far too long for a recovery from a hernia operation, and he would like me to return to work ASAP. I asked him to put that in writing while I waited downstairs in the operations center. He then informed me he would not do this and ordered me to get out of his office.

I did not hear a peep from that little man in the next two weeks before returning to work at Tampa Airport. It was good to be seeing all the Delta gang again after six months. Nikki was also glad to see me go back to work since this would give her some breathing space especially as she had just discovered she was pregnant.

It was nineteen seventy one and Nikki was beaming through her pregnancy with our daughter Julliet. The pregnancy was a difficult one, restricting our travel to England to participate in the christening of Ro and John's quintuplets. Ro was holding Gary for us to be his godparents. Early in January we were so surprised to hear a knock at our door—it was Ro and John visiting us, leaving their five babies in England, for a much-needed break. We were living on Leone Avenue in South Tampa. Ro and Nikki visited while John and I played golf. We did take them to Sunday lunch at my parents for a Southern feast of fried chicken with all the fixings. During the past two years, we had visited them several times in England, and we could not get over five small kids being potty trained at one time! We stayed on Leone Avenue for another two years, and our traveling was curtailed except for going back to England to visit Grandma and PaPa. Julliet was born at Tampa General Hospital on February 12, 1971.

After Julliet was born, we started looking for a three-bedroom, two-bath house. We sold the house on Leona Avenue for a three/two on Fair Oaks. Nikki no longer worked as a schoolteacher, and we talked about doing something else that would give us the freedom to travel or enable us to use the travel to start a business. Since we went to England often, we could bring antiques back and sell them on El Prado Boulevard. We both toured nearby antique shops asking the various shop owners what they could use from London. There was interest in small items such as silver, brass, all types of wood boxes, or anything decorative. It was so much fun turning our vacations visiting Nikki's parents into buying trips.

After two years of selling out of our suitcases, we opened up an antique shop. We had been to England this time for three weeks to buy enough for a twenty-foot sea freight container. We rented a small panel van to travel out to the country surrounding Harrow and London where the antiques were cheaper. The farther we were from any built-up areas, the better it was. Nikki's mother, Flo, would baby-sit Julliet to give us the freedom to start this exciting endeavor.

After two weeks we started painting our name, "Law Antiques," on the building. The container arrived with much fanfare through advertising and word of mouth. The owners of the Golden Eagle Antique Shop, Angie with her husband, Jim, helped us to price our goods so we could sell them quickly and go back to England for another buying trip.

I was still working at Delta and loving my job with all the benefits that came with it. Julliet and the shop kept Nikki busy, but Julliet was an easy child to look after in a playpen. Then Jonathan came along on June 6, 1974. We stayed in the house on Fair Oaks for another two years. Then Nikki fell in love with an English Tudor–style two-story home with an extra lot where the children could play, on San Pedro in a better area of South Tampa closer to Beach Park. Our house sold quickly, and Nikki was able to put an offer on the house on San Pedro. After moving into the new house we found out the neighbor across the street was Jodi Mace, a single lady who also worked for Delta on the ticket counter.

By this time, our friends from Delta, and Lee had two children, Lee Anne and Mary. They were two beautiful little girls. The Palevedas had three children; all our friends families were growing in numbers.

**

Raising and schooling our children, Nikki was content, but after eleven years with Delta, I wanted something more. We talked about immigrating back to the UK so that

Nikki's mom could see Julliet and Jonathan grow up. Nikki's dad had passed away a few years earlier; the day we got the news, I was recovering from a vasectomy I had had done the day before. Nikki answered the phone, and Flo said she needed to speak to me. After hanging the phone up, I broke the news to Nikki. She took it hard. Delta flew us to England immediately, and Bill Ryal told me, "Lloyd, however long it takes, stay in England and take care of Nikki and her Mother on Delta's time." What a wonderful friend and supervisor he was.

Since starting with Delta Airlines, we had probably flown the Atlantic twenty times. The first ten years we took numerous trips to visit Ro and John, or I would meet up with John in Toronto on a business trip. How we all loved the proper British way of eating and acting on our best behavior.

This would go on with Delta for another two and a half years. But in January 1981, we decided to give up our life in the USA and move to Grantham, England. Most of 1980 was taken getting resident status for the children and me. April 5, 1981, was the big move. Nikki was very apprehensive about this life-changing decision, and we both were scared a little because Delta Air Lines was our security.

The day we shipped out on Delta to England was extremely emotionally difficult. There had to have been twenty cardboard boxes, Delta garment boxes, or hatboxes, plus another four suitcases to be checked in. We were fortunate to sell practically everything we owned at the garage sale during the previous three days. We sold the house for a good profit, and our total cash to emigrate with was fifty thousand dollars.

We arrived at Flo's in Grantham safely. The excitement of being self-employed was good. Flo was enjoying the children and Nikki. Maybe this was not a financially good move, but the thought of Nikki's mother watching her grandchildren grow up was worth the gamble. Two months went by, and we lay in bed talking about where we could look for a place to live and set up a business. Before we left Tampa, Clara and Peter—two expatriates—told us they wanted to open an antique shop as partners in Tampa, which gave us a head start for starting an antique exporting company.

During the third month, we found an old shop with living accommodations above and with a nice-size barn. It was called Dracus Cottage in Hagworthingham, Lincolnshire. The price was twenty-four thousand pounds, or thirty-two thousand dollars. We put half down with the rest to be paid in twelve months. We bought a small panel van, and we were in business. We started attending local auctions and estate farm sales. Furniture was cheap, and we could fill a twenty-foot container for eight thousand dollars. We started shipping containers to our partners in Tampa that summer; we were up and running! This was so exciting, to be free from constraints of going to work at Delta.

That fall, Flo sold her house and moved in with us. She handed Nikki a ten-thousand-pound check, or about fourteen thousand dollars, as part of her inheritance. Flo still had enough money in her bank account for luxuries plus her fags, as she called her cigarettes.

That first year, many Delta friends visited us in Hagworthyham, including Lee and Jimetta Anderson and their children. They brought with them Julliet's bicycle, first on the plane then on the train to Grantham. They also brought some of Jonathan's things we'd left behind at their house in North Tampa.

Winter was starting in and we had to put in central heating—Dracus Cottage was cold. Nikki was worried one night during a blizzard because I had left with Rodney Chesterton to buy furniture in Scotland; we traveled on the train from Lincoln Station and arrived back at Goltho Hall where Rodney's wife, Jane, was waiting for us. Jane had also been worried that we were going to be cut off by the blizzard. I called Nikki to tell her that it should be OK to drive home. Nikki called the publican, Mick, who practically ran the village, to tell him of my plans. He said the snowplow would meet me in Horncastle and plow a way through. Thank God Nikki got everything arranged. The snow was so thick it was like driving in a thick fog. I still remember my heart beating very fast. I got home safely; then we were snowed in for three days. "Hags," as the locals called it, was completely cut off. Hot mince pies with cups of tea went down well. The local post office and shop was attached to our place and was the social club where everyone met, so Nikki was entertaining our neighbors for most of three days. She reveled in the togetherness of it all.

In fact, Nikki always made sure that our social life in Hags was full. We all went to church most Sundays. The village church was built over seven hundred years ago; it was made of local stone and was very beautiful. It was also very cold. Between the church, the pub, and the local school with its plays and pantomimes along with work, we were kept busy.

The next summer, Clifford Hall Jones came into our workshop. He was organizing a party to celebrate Charles and Diana's wedding down at the local school. In his posh public-school accent, he said to Nikki and me, "Having lived in America, would you two be proficient enough to organize a barbeque for the village on the Saturday after next?" He thought there would be at least 140 residents maybe more attending. We said, "Sure." Clifford would have to collect a pound from each one attending, along with their names. One English pound per person would be sufficient for the meat and the veggies. Kelsey, the local butcher, provided the sausages, wings, and chicken thighs very cheaply.

David Grey, Andy, and Pete all helped with de-barking an old giant dead oak tree for the fuel. We built a twenty-five-foot grill on top of stones. It was a fantastic night; we were brought so many beers that there were eleven beers in a row waiting for us to consume The next day, Sunday, everyone told us how much they had all enjoyed the food and the atmosphere. Never before was there a gathering in memory in Hagworthingham this enjoyable.

Some time later, Nikki was reading a real-estate magazine and saw a mansion for sale in Scotland, forty-three rooms at the top of a glen with a valley below and a large trout stream meandering through the glen. She made an appointment the next Saturday to view it. We fell in love with Glen Markie Lodge and put in an offer that day. We moved in thirty days later, so it was off to Scotland with Nikki, Julliet, and Jonathan, Nikki's mother, me, the dog, the cat, and seven kittens.

Winter came in as the Bevans—Nikki's childhood friend, Jacque, and her husband, David—were going home to Heathersage, Derbyshire, after spending the holidays with us. We took them to the Dundee station on New Year's Eve, dog and all. I barely made it back up the mountain when it started to snow, snow, and snow. We did make it out three weeks later and bought a side of beef from the local butcher in Alyth. It was enough provision for a month. Then the snow started again on January 25, and it never stopped snowing until the first of April. We didn't see the car or the Land Rover for two months!

Mike and Myra Messiter, our only neighbors behind us, were our saving grace. Mike, now a retired 757 captain with British Airways, had snowshoes. When he was home, he would walk to the village for milk and the mail. After he made four trips, Nikki said to him, "Lloyd will do the trip next Tuesday." Our driveway was over three miles long up the Glen and the mountain, so it took me over eight hours to go down to the village because the snow was waist deep and I had no proper snowshoes. The snowdrifts were up to ten feet high during the worst blizzards. Glen Shee Ski Resort could be closed sometimes for weeks. My mom, who hardly ever phoned, called to see if we were all right since the news about our winter reached the networks in the States with skiers cut off for quite a while.

After that one episode when I thought it could not get any worse, we ran out of coal. Every day our goal was to find and cut up fallen tree limbs that were under the ice and snow, and store them in the stable for fuel. The kids would ski every day for hours because they only went to school six days in three months.

We had bought this house with overdraft funds because we could still not sell our house in England. It was worth it because Nikki and I both shared this dream of owning a mansion. I had no work for three months, and our overdraft hit fifty-seven thousand pounds. K.C. Jones, the bank manager from Spillsby, Lincolnshire, called to say we had sixty days to come up with the funds or they would take both houses. When Nikki and I needed to talk about difficult problems we always took long walks; good news waited until baths were drawn. Then we would have a cup of tea or coffee and work out whatever it was. Most of the time, it would be about our business or finances, good or bad. This time, we decided to sell the Scottish mansion, as much as we loved it.

We talked the manager into giving us 120 days, and the next week we signed up with a property agent in Blairgowrie. They told us that to sell such a substantial house like ours it would have to be advertised properly. We gave them an overdraft check for two thousand pounds, and seventy days later, we had only one couple interested in our mansion. Thank God they wanted it.

We sold it and doubled our money in less than two years. Three weeks later we sold the home in Hagworthingham and paid off the overdraft with lots of money to spare. The new owner's stipulation on buying the lodge was that we had to stay on as caretakers for another twelve months. They were from the Tyne and Ware area and would move in the next year. Hooray! Nikki was so happy. The business was building up, and I met new clients.

We moved out of Glen Markie Lodge into another stately home, Ruthven Mill. We signed a five-year lease and with the money we had left started our wholesale warehouse business in Brandon, Florida. That was a bad venture. We had three different managers and lost everything by 1987. We closed down the business and arrived back in Scotland broke. Again I took long walks with Nikki and told her if we really worked hard, we could pay of the eighteen-thousand-dollar overdraft. Our monthly house and living expenses were still over two thousand pounds a month. But one year later we had no debts and our income started to grow again.

During our time in Scotland, we made lots of friends. Some would accompany us to Florida for a holiday every winter, such as Jim and Jeanette McGill and Harry and Rosemary Sudron, who lived just down the river from us in separate old grist mills. On all of our trips to Florida from Scotland in the 1980s, we would spend at least a month in the sun to recharge our bodies and minds.

On one of our winter Florida trips, we received a phone call from Steve Rothrock, a customer and a friend. He said he was sending his plane down to Tampa to pick Nikki, Jonathan, and me up for a three-day trip to Georgetown, South Carolina, to discuss a business venture. That Friday, at lunchtime, Steve's pilot met us at the executive side airport, which was part of the Tampa International Airport. When we took off, I was sitting in the copilot seat. After about thirty minutes, I went back to see Nikki. After another thirty minutes, the pilot asked me to come back to the cockpit. He needed help and as I sat down he asked me to get out the airport manual. We had to divert since the right engine had quit. As I was looking for landing coordinates for Myrtle Beach, I looked for the engine gauge in the instrument panel and noticed the right engine was showing no fuel. I told the pilot, and he said, "Thank God!" He started the engine after pulling a switch.

But this flying episode wasn't over, unfortunately. On approach to Georgetown Airport, it was very foggy. The pilot couldn't see the runway and as he turned around after missing the approach, he asked me to time him for one minute once we started over the sea. As we went out for another approach, I asked him what the minimum was for that airport. He told me seven hundred feet. But how could that be, I asked, since these trees were less than forty feet tall? He said there was a five-hundred-foot brick smokestack in line with the runway. I could not talk him into going to Myrtle Beach; he said it would be OK and asked me to look out for a small pond. As we were getting close, I soon saw a pond. He moved the plane to the right and pushed the wheel quickly to go for the landing. Thank God it was the right pond!

We were all shaken, Nikki especially. Three days later, Steve picked us up for the ride back to Tampa, but Nikki informed him and me that she had made reservations to fly back from Charlestown on a commercial jet. Three hundred dollars later, it was good to get back to Indian Shores Beach after almost not being on this planet. Nikki was never again to travel on a small plane.

For the rest of our holiday, Nikki, Jim and Jeanette would do the *Daily Telegraph* crossword puzzle while my time was spent playing golf or fishing. We had one last get-together with the entire Delta group out of Tampa before flying back to Scotland. We were not looking forward to the weather back in Alyth or Ruthven. We arrived in Gatwick cold and tired, ready for the all-day train ride up to the station in Perth. The train was warm enough for us all to sleep, read the paper, have a cup of tea, and go back to sleep again. By the time we arrived in Perth, we had been on the train ten hours out of a total of twenty-seven hours traveling. It was dark, cold, and wet. At least Ruthven Mill would be warm and toasty; we thought that we might have to turn the electric blanket on.

Lloyd the soldier 1966

John & Ro's wedding 1966

Lloyd & Nikki's wedding 1967

Lloyd & Nikki's wedding, group picture

Ro & John back from Seattle 1967

Mom, dad & babies 1970

Early 1970 the babies

The christening 1970 - nursery nurses Sheila & Susan, Ro's mum Vera, John, Ro, & Doris Letts

The babies 1ˢᵗ birthday

Ro, John, Nikki & Lloyd at Gertha's pad Florida 1970

Ro, John & the quintuplets 1972 Chorleywood

Backyard at Longhope 1973

Magazine article 1

THURSDAY, SEPT. 14, 1972

The Letts family on parade for Citizen photographer Barrie Pope

The Letts Quins make it
a busy life for Mother

THE Letts Quins took a little finding in their new home at Nupend Lodge, Longhope, but when the right gate was eventually opened it was quite obvious that the search was over.

For there was Tanya—or was it Cara? — thumping the family Dormobile with a rubber mallet, and there was Sharon —or was it Joanne?—looking on with interest.

And sounds from within, and the array of toys fastened around the door, were a give-away for the rest of the tribe.

The "Lett Quins" Memory is notoriously short but it was only just over two years ago—in December 1969—that Mrs. Rosemary Letts made her own special claim to fame by giving birth to sextuplets.

One baby was still-born. The other five are very much alive and kicking, thank you.

Since they came to Longhope about the end of July they have frequently been cited about the village. Come to think of it, it would be difficult to miss them, and it is going to be quite an occasion, and a substantial boost in numbers, when the time comes for them to start at the village school.

Why have the Letts family moved from their home at Chorley Woods, Herts, and

why should they come to Longhope?

Mr. John Letts (27) to The Citizen: "We had to move for financial reasons; we just could not afford to live in the London area.

"We looked over a wide area of England for a suitable house, but at that time there was only the choice of two or three houses at the right price in this whim of the country.

"This was the pick of the bunch. It suits us very well at the moment, we like it here, and perhaps our one regret is that we have had to leave behind so many of our friends."

Attractive looking Mrs. Rosemary Letts (26), a long way removed from the picture of a harassed mother of five,

by Alec Spencer

pointed out that the quins too had fallen in love with their new home.

"They like the house itself, the large garden is ideal because at our last place we didn't have much of a garden, and they are fascinated by the donkey just on up the lane.

"I think that the whole area is a splendid one for children.

"Since we came to Longhope we have had nothing but friendliness and kindness from local people and from the tradesmen.

"They have not pushed themselves but have been only too willing to help out if needed."

And both Mr. and Mrs. Letts made it quite clear that they had not moved to Longhope because they were fed up with the Press and publicity. In all that had been written there was only one article that had given a completely wrong impression and which they had taken exception to.

Asked if the bringing up of five children had led to any particular problem, Mrs. Letts said: "Not enough time."

"It is a hard grind morning to night," she said, "and now it is very rarely that we get a night without some-one waking up between mid-night and six o'clock.

"Fortunately we have had little or no illness although Gary—the only boy—had a throat infection the other week.

"But now they have got past the baby stage they wake up and ask for things like a drink of water and strangely enough our nights have become more disturbed."

Mrs. Letts said that all five children had completely different personalities.

Magazine article 2

The Delta house Feb. 1975

Chapter 9

Longhope to Hopeless

Ro's Story

The kids were now two years old, and moving day came. The BBC filmed it all, and as John was to say years later, so started two of the best years of our life. There was no more help; we were on our own and we loved it. We got into quite a routine; when the weather was good, John would work outside, often while looking after the kids. When the weather didn't permit, he would paint and fix the inside of the house. I did all the meals apart from one day a week when I got a day off. Mostly I would drive into town and go shopping, and in the evening, John not only got the kids tea but also our dinner. The menu was always the same—cheese soufflé with spinach. It was delicious! It was not the easiest thing to cook, but John had found the recipe and had it down pat. The spinach was fresh from the garden. In return, he got a day off to play golf each weekend. John always played with Bob Howells, who lived in Cinderford, the next village to ours. Bob and his lovely wife, Eileen, were our closest friends while we lived in Longhope. I still treasure Bob's friendship today; unfortunately Eileen died a number of years ago from mouth cancer.

Gradually the house grew on me. John was right; he knew I would love it once it was clean and painted. The kids enjoyed the garden and the surrounding countryside. There was a donkey up the lane, and there were cows and a bull in the field next to us. The BBC still came—but less often now. The documentary was almost finished. We did get visits from the grandparents and our friends some weekends, but for the most part we were on our own. Quite often we'd take a family trip. All of us would pile into the V.W. bus and go to the zoo, to a park, or to whatever was going on locally. We really got very efficient and things ran pretty smoothly. I never dealt with the finances nor wanted to, but I thought we were keeping afloat. I wish now that John had shared more of that responsibility with me, but because he wanted to protect me, he took it all on himself.

The documentary about our family was called *Quite a Family* and was shown on TV in 1973. We were pleased with it, for the most part. During the final interview we were quite stressed, though, and I wouldn't say the same things now that I did then. There was so much footage that had to be left out. All those hours of filming over three years were taken down to less than sixty minutes. We were told we'd get everything from the cutting room floor, but we never did.

The kids were nearly four now, and everything seemed OK until, suddenly in 1973, our accountant died. John was quite concerned and started to talk about what we should do next. We had always thought that at some point, we would like to go back to Seattle, but by then they had tightened up immigration laws; and without a job or a lot of money, we would never be accepted.

While we were in Seattle, we had visited Vancouver a number of times. We had liked it a lot, so John started looking into immigrating to Canada. Before long, the house was up for sale. John had finished all the painting and fixing up. He was also a talented gardener so the yard was lovely, including a large tree house he made for all the kids. I was sad at the thought of leaving Nupend Lodge but at the same time excited at the thought of a new adventure. My poor mum and dad were going to lose not a daughter but a whole family this time.

As it turned out, we only had one serious buyer, but that was all we needed. The house sold for thirty thousand pounds, and we felt that was a reasonable profit in just two years. As soon as the sale was final, it was a matter of selling most of the house's contents and packing up the rest, only keeping things of sentimental value.

The evening before the garage sale, John went out with the boys from the golf club for a farewell drink. It must have been a very good night because he was not in a state to help me the next morning. I had five four-year-olds running around and a hoard of people responding to the advertisement in the paper for a moving sale. Some people took advantage and stuff got taken without payment, but there was nothing I could do about it. In the great scheme of things, it didn't make too much difference.

Granny Letts had agreed to look after Sharon, Joanne, and Tanya for a month so that we could get to Vancouver, buy a house, get settled, and be ready for them to follow. Looking back, that was quite remarkable of her; we could not have managed the move without her help. I was exhausted by the time we got to the airport: John, me, Cara and Gary. All I remember of that flight is saying, "Yes, I'll have a martini, please," thinking it was just the vermouth. I sometimes drank it on the rocks, but never with gin! I had a couple of sips and passed out. The next thing I heard over the intercom was the stewardess asking if there was an MD on board who could attend to me.

I slept my way across the Atlantic, and when we arrived in Vancouver I was put in a wheelchair and given priority through immigration. John had to cope with two four-year-olds, luggage, and a very frail wife. I was only 105 pounds at that time, and moving countries with all that involved was taking its toll. The four of us got to Surrey, British Columbia, and rented a motel cabin for a few weeks. Nikki and Lloyd came to visit us there, and so did our friends John and Jean from Seattle. It all looked a bit grim, but it was the early days.

We managed to find a house to buy in Delta, not far away; it was already empty so we got moved in and furnished it within that one-month time slot. Granny Letts arrived with Sharon, Joanne, and Tanya and stayed to help us for a few weeks. It was lovely to have the family all together again, and we felt optimistic about the future.

John started to look for work. He wanted to get back into the computer industry. The bulk of our money had to be left in England for four years, so John walked around all of the banks asking for a loan against it. They all said no except the Bank of Nova Scotia. Thank goodness for that, or I'm not sure what we would have done. That was one good thing, but there were still no job offers. I remember John saying one day, "Tomorrow I'm going to McDonald's to get a job; we need some money coming in."

Amazingly, the very next day, John got a call from Hewlett Packard to go for an interview, and he got the job as a salesman. It was a huge relief! John soon made his mark in the company and became one of their top salesmen. I could never quite understand him in that role because he was soft-spoken and not at all pushy, but he explained to me that his job was to help people improve their businesses and their lives. Then it all made sense. He had a very gentle manner that people liked.

Now we had time to look for a better house with more room and a larger yard. In 1975, and we moved to Seventy-sixth Avenue on the border of Surrey and Langley. It was a five-bedroom ranch on an acre with a huge family room off of the kitchen—how happy I was! The family who lived opposite us was Kathy and Glen Delair and their three boys, who were between six and ten years old. We became great friends during the nine-plus years we lived in that house. There were many evenings when the four of us would sit on the porch having a drink while all the kids played together.

John was always thinking of ways to make money. He tried another small business from home, something to do with calculating mortgages. That didn't work out either, but it was good experience, just preparation for things to come.

The kids were growing up fast. Now they were helping with chores and settling down well in school. It costs a lot of money to raise five children, so I thought it was time to get a job myself. I'd had a background in hairdressing, so I applied at Raymond Salon, a chain that operated in the Woodward's Department stores, as a receptionist/assistant manager. The area manager told me later that I got the job because if I could organize a family of five seven-year-olds, I should be able to run the salon. I really enjoyed getting out of the house, and I loved the Woodward's store. It sold everything, even had a really good grocery department, which I frequented almost every day before I came home. Working at Raymond's as a hairdresser was another English girl, Linda Shigamatsu. Her accent was identical to mine, and it turned out that we were born within a couple of streets of each other in Watford. We have been friends ever since.

John and I had to be very organized at home to make it all work. I always made the five school lunches the night before. The kids took turns to clear the dishes, and they all had a room to clean on the weekends. Every one of them hated it, and I was probably too particular. It makes life hard if one's too much of a perfectionist.

John helped whenever he could, especially on Saturdays when I always worked. He would get Kaiser buns, black forest ham, and cheese; it never changed. He loved being outdoors, and there was always work to do—plus now we had acquired three cats, two large dogs, and some rabbits. John still played golf whenever he could, and I was happy he did. He had an awful lot of responsibility, which was about to increase in a big way when he quit Hewlett Packard and started "Letts Marketing," a small computer consulting business. He was a great thinker, and I always believed he was destined to be successful.

Our parents came out every other year, and we went back to England the alternate years. My dad was wonderful in keeping in close contact with the kids. He would do audiotapes, talking to them all individually, as well as lots of letter writing. It really was rewarding, and I think all of the children felt very close to Granddad Egerton and still remember him as a very strong, positive influence in their lives.

John and I used to do tapes back then as well. John would talk into the machine as he drove to work. He'd talk about what he was seeing out the window and what his plans for the future were. Dad wrote us long, weekly letters. He was a very interesting man, with an inquiring mind, and until a few days before he died he was reading and learning new things.

In 1979, John's brother, Geoff, and his girlfriend, Di, came to Canada for the oldest brother Pete's wedding in Ottawa. Afterwards, they came across Canada to visit us. They were going through tumultuous times in their private lives back in England, and were both interested in the new life we had in B.C. They thought it might work for them.

The following year, Geoff and Di emigrated with their four kids, two each from previous marriages, all under ten. They came to stay with us for three months, so we had four adults and nine kids to feed every day—quite a challenge! But I remember the time fondly. We did the meals in two shifts, the kids first, and then after that was cleared away we were able to enjoy our own supper. Everyone pitched in, and John and I were delighted to have them over in Canada with us. With the Delair family across the road and their three boys, we had some very good times.

In 1980, Nikki, Lloyd, and their two children—Julliet, nine, and Jonathan, seven—came to visit us. My kids were ten, so they had good fun together, and we took them to Stanley Park, the Capillano Suspension Bridge, and up Grouse Mountain. One night we got a sitter in and the four of us went for dinner at the Cannery, a wonderful seafood restaurant on the water, which unfortunately closed a few years ago.

Letts Marketing was doing well enough to expand. It became Northwest Digital, and John took several employees from Hewlett Packard to join the company. In fact, two of them became business partners, and the goal was to eventually put the company on the Toronto Stock Exchange.

John worked extremely hard, and the business did well. He opened offices in several other provinces. This meant that he had to travel quite a bit. Once in early 1981, when he went to Toronto, he asked Lloyd to join him for dinner. Lloyd was working for Delta Airlines and could fly first class for nothing. Nikki and I talked on the phone about it and wondered just how good a time those guys were having!

In 1982, suddenly there was an economic meltdown. Interest rates soared, and John's business was in danger of going under. He had to lay off quite few people, close some of the offices, and put others on part-time. John was under a lot of stress, but he kept most of it inside; he always wanted to shield me from worry. He'd tell me that I had enough to deal with, five kids, the pets, the house, and a job. Throughout all this time we managed to enjoy a good social life. We'd both made friends at work and always looked forward to getting a baby-sitter and going out with them.

John and I always wanted the kids to have their own individual identities, so we thought it might be a good idea to put Cara and Gary in a different school. That did not work out well; they were very unhappy. After that they all attended the same school for the next few years. All five children had pretty good report cards. Cara and Gary were both artistic, but Gary lost interest as he grew up. Cara is a renowned artist today, although she has to supplement her income with managing a restaurant. It was a challenge to get Gary to do his homework, but he was a good boy most of the time. Today, like his dad, his talent is with computers. Tanya was the most academic, quite a bit ahead of the rest, but when she was a teenager, life got in the way and we'll never know what heights she might have climbed to; things have been difficult for her, but her talent still shows through in her poetry and writing. Cara, Sharon, and Jo were all bright and hardworking as children. They kept that ethic through their lives and have proved to be wonderful mothers and kind, generous people. Cara always seemed to be the leader of the pack, and she was my biggest supporter during the tough times. But I want to say how proud I am of them all and how dearly I love them. Maybe I should have let them know that a little more through the years.

My dad had a brilliant mind and was passionate about politics. He would have loved me to share that interest, but my love was for animals. Thank goodness John became the son he had never had, and they had many happy discussions putting the country and the world to right.

I always looked forward to my weekly phone calls with Nikki. She'd keep me up to date with what was happening in their lives and our friends in England. I'd likewise tell her if I heard from Pauline or Daphne and all the ups and downs that we were having. This was about the time John started to complain about stomach pains and was given medication for heartburn and indigestion.

Geoff and Di moved into Fort Langley with their four kids, and when Granddad Letts died, Granny emigrated and bought a mobile home in a park a few miles away. We felt lucky to have most of the family close by, but life can only stay that good for so long. The kids were now fifteen, and things started to get difficult at home. They were acting like typical teenagers, and most of the discipline was left to me, John was so busy at work; he was spending more and more time there, and it never occurred to me that someone else might be taking care of him better than I was. One day, almost out of the blue, John gave me the choice of staying in the house with three of kids or moving out with two. At first it was on the pretense of us needing space, but I soon realized that there was more to it. We found a townhouse by Guilford Town Centre in Surrey for Cara, Sharon, and me. It would be a little closer to my work, but the girls would have to go to a new school. That was hard for them and they never did like it. John would pay all the bills plus expenses for Cara and Sharon.

Our eighteenth wedding anniversary was a day of despair for me. When John said that he did not want to celebrate it at all, I knew I had lost him. It was an absolutely devastating feeling, and I cried all night. He could not handle a woman being too emotional, so I was probably driving him further away. I was working full-time now, and Cara and Sharon were a great support. Cara got into baking, and it was a great comfort to come home to her cheese puffs and have a glass of wine.

John dropped in fairly often to have a cup of tea and see how we were doing. I decided to be strong and optimistic about things from now on. We started to have some good conversations again and not just talk about problems, especially regarding the kids. John wanted to meet me in the pub across the street from Woodward's one evening after work. A feeling I had told me that it was important, so I took extra care in getting ready. The girls at work helped me with my hair and makeup, and John was sitting at a small table when I got there.

Somehow the old magic came back that night. After the pub, we went to an Italian restaurant and had a lovely meal. By the end of the evening we knew we were together again. John told me later that he had planned to ask me for a divorce that night and tell me about his new relationship, but thank goodness that never happened.

He also told me later about a certain night when I had tried to call him at work because there had been a heavy snowfall, and I was worried about driving home. He did not return the call because he was with that certain someone. I had no choice but to drive. I was terrified, especially crossing a busy bridge in those conditions in the dark. Despite shaking like a leaf the whole way, I made it back to the townhouse. John told me that he had felt enormous guilt that night (and probably other nights, too, but that one in particular). For me, it was a valuable driving lesson, and I was a lot more confident after that.

John had been having stomach problems for a while, and the medications he was taking were not helping. The doctor thought it might be a stress-induced ulcer, so he got the necessary tests scheduled.

During the few short months of the separation, I never could pluck up the courage to tell Mum and Dad, I did not want to break their hearts, especially Dad's. So every Sunday when I used to call them, I'd rush over to the other house, about a twenty-two-minute drive away, and make the phone call from there. Much later, when John and I were back together, I told them all about it. The kids sixteenth birthday arrived and we were a family again, despite living in two separate homes. We all felt a lot happier.

Chapter 10

Back to Work

Lloyd's Story

Waiting for us at home in our mail was a contract to supply an Australian auction house with containers of antiques to be paid for through a bank clearinghouse in London. This was a good start to a new year. The next day Nikki was planning my workload out for the year; along with the American Antique dealers we were going to be on the road a lot buying enough to supply at least forty containers for the next fifty-two weeks. We had to have someone pick up purchases from Glasgow, Perth, Dundee, Inverness, and the middle part of England. Richard Thompson Removals was out of Blairgowrie, where Julliet went to high school. Richard's wife, Christine, taught school there. We all were busy that year, and Julliet was studying for her final exams and staying in her room to study most of the time. Also, being a teenager, she didn't mix much except with her friends on weekends. She also had a waitressing job at Alyth golf club where my son, Jonathan, and I were members; we became friends socially and in business with the Thompsons. Richard also had a huge furniture van large enough to move fifteen tons of all types of furniture including pianos.

Nikki thought we should hire someone to help load our containers. Our container sales that year had reached forty-five: thirty to America and fifteen to Australia. Friends of ours, Basil and Joy, were antique dealers from Somerset, and they agreed to hire on for at least a year. They also were to live on the Isla River where they bought a beautiful house by the Ruthven Bridge. They became participants in our social life with barbecues and dinners at the golf club.

Nikki had seen a Jaguar, British racing green, in a dealership in Kirriemuir. She took me to see it. They wanted our Volvo as a trade in plus three thousand pounds in cash. It was too good of a deal to pass up. The Jag was so comfortable that we could visit all the auction houses from Blairgowrie to Perth to Inverness and then go back toward Aberdeen where we left bids in Forest, Elgin, Keith, and Montrose. We still felt pretty good riding in the Jag all day. This was the best part of our business; all we did was to spend other people's money! The business grew to about one million dollars in purchases per year. Our commission was approximately 10 percent per container, and all of the expenses were built into the purchases. That way our combined salary was one hundred thousand dollars a year after expenses.

We would always leave bids instead of attending the auctions. Our bids were always under the value of what we would pay so if the auction ran us up to our maximum bid we could still add enough to cover all expenses so it would not matter. Richard would pick up on the same route every two weeks.

Taylor of Montrose was a mega auction house sometimes having two or three auctioneers going at the same time. This was also every two weeks. We had the weekends free to socialize, or Jonathan and I would play golf. Julliet waited tables at the golf course. Nikki stayed home to do her crossword and call her many childhood friends along with the American friends still working for Delta. Our phone bill in the 1980s was always three hundred pounds a month, approximately four hundred and fifty dollars. Most often when we had clients or friends staying with us, we would take them to eat at the golf club. This was the only time Julliet's tips were good; usually our Delta friends were very generous.

Our Scottish friends who always accompanied us to Florida, Jim, Jeanette, Harry, Rosemary, and Richard and Christine Thompson, and our lovely French friend, Mary France and her husband, Gustof, a Norwegian ski instructor up at Glenshee, all loved to party together, along with Nikki's cousins from England. Jacque and David Bevans were frequent visitors, too, and then Nikki and the kids would go to visit everyone during the summer. Our get-togethers at Ruthven Mill were wonderful. Many Delta airlines friends and their spouses plus children would fly over to stay with us. It seemed like we were always busy, living a type of privileged, Victorian lifestyle. The McGills, friends and fellow antique dealers from Scotland, staged either murder-mystery weekends or fancy dress parties with loads of other Delta friends. I remember Dale and Mary Boyette, Dick and Melanie Daniels, and our old friends, Lee and Jimetta Anderson, at the McGills' for one of these murder-mystery parties; Dale was dressed up like a French naval officer. We did party a lot—spring was the start of it all, and it carried on until the fall.

Nikki opened an antique shop on the green in Blairgowrie, and Jeanette, Jim and Harry all had antique shops in Alyth We still had many, many socials, and our American clients came to stay at Ruthven Mill. It was a very impressive place, dating back to the seventeen hundreds. Nikki and I loved it there, and Ro and John visited us there along with countless others. Yet again, another decision had to be made. We did not want to leave Florida so soon after only a month. Flying back to Scotland in February of 1990, after a couple of scotches, Nikki said, "We will move back." I could commute every seven weeks; we could save money since the warehouse had a kitchen, bathroom, and an office for a bedroom. Ruthven Mill was costing us two thousand pounds a month, nearly three thousand dollars.

So we moved back to Florida. We brought Jonathan over for his junior year at Chamberlin High School, where he made the varsity golf team. Julliet was going to university in the UK, so Nikki and I would commute for the next fifteen years to Scotland.

We moved the business, Anglo American Antique Exporters, to the Newark/Grantham area to be closer to the mega antiques fairs like Swinderby and Newark. Back in Tampa we bought a house in the Forest Hills area on Babe Zaharias Golf Course with owner financing. Because we had lived in the United Kingdom for so many years, we had no credit history in the States. After twenty months there, Nikki wanted to move and open an antique warehouse in Hayesville, North Carolina. We had scoped it out three times previously. Jim and Jeanette went with us on one of the trips within the three-month period; every time we were there it was foggy and cold, not like Florida, which was bright and always sunny. Nikki was adamant this would be a good opportunity, especially since Jonathan had graduated from high school and was hanging with undesirable friends and getting into under-age drinking and social drugs. We found out later that he would travel with high school friends to an area in Tampa that was known for buying drugs and alcoholic items. So we moved again, after selling our lovely pool home. Living in Tampa we had been almost neighbors with our friends from Delta: Lee and Jimetta, and Ed and Phyllis. We'd had plenty of visitors from England and America in that house, too, particularly Jacque and David Bevan. We often had a house full with lots of barbecues with the entire Delta group joining us. But it was time to leave, and this was another move that turned out to be fabulous.

Nikki and I went to England in May of 1993 to buy a container to sell wholesale to dealers in the tri-state area of North Carolina, Georgia, and Tennessee. We sold the container in an empty store in Hayesville, North Carolina, and made a decent profit. Nikki was optimistic that we could find a store close to Lake Chatuge or Lake Nottely. She found an old general store on the corner of Nottely Dam Road and Murphy Highway, halfway between Blairsville, Georgia, and Murphy, North Carolina. It was the old Poteet's Store. We rented it from Billy and Barbara Poteet and their sons Larry, Jimmy, and Marty. They were all ex–US Marines like their dad. Barbara was a nice person and Nikki liked her a lot, though she couldn't understand Billy and Larry; their accents were very Southern so I had to be the interpreter. Nikki said that if Billy and Larry would open their mouths when they spoke she might have a chance to decipher their words.

We rented a house on Lake Vista Drive and lived there for one year. We met John and Susan Wade, Geoff and Cathy Jones, Jean Cook, and Lyn and Barry Varian. We all have been very good friends for many years. Like everyone else, they all wondered what Nikki ever saw in me. I was lucky she had seen something.

We opened the new antique shop in the spring of 1995. Business was good from the start. Nikki was astonished that stained-glass windows reclaimed from old building sites in England were so popular. We started selling furniture and bric-a-brac, but the windows were the best moneymaker. We were selling fifty windows a week at forty dollars each, paying only ten dollars each in England. We stayed there for two years. Jonathan had started school at Western North Carolina close to Silva. By this time we needed a larger warehouse. After a month or so looking we found the Old Skating Rink in Blue Ridge, Georgia, for rent. It was another lake town in the Blue Ridge Mountains. Julliet came to see us taking a break from her studies at Newcastle University in England. She had grown up so much, was looking beautiful, and was very confident in herself.

Jonathan was in a dorm at the university, and Julliet went over one Friday night to stay with him. She came back on Saturday to tell her mom to get him away from that dorm; he was into drugs and not going to classes, just getting by on the allowance we gave him so he could study and not worry about working a part-time job. I was to leave in one week to load a container in Scotland for two different clients, so I asked Jonathan if he wanted to go with me so he could help and then stay on to visit his friends. He jumped at the chance. We left out of Atlanta to fly to Gatwick; on the plane I told Jonathan I had bought him a one-way ticket and he was to attend Aberdeen University, thinking that drugs were too hard to get in the UK. He was accepted as an overseas student on a four-year course. We found out later he attended the first day of each year then did nothing the rest of the time. He never wanted to get a job. Each month he was costing us more than seven hundred dollars in room and board. Looking back, he just conned us so he could live a fun by life doing nothing. He would drink most days with his friends. I found out later that we had been supporting him for thirty months without Jonathan ever telling us that he was not attending university. It felt like someone stealing from your hard-earned wages. I finally flew over to confront him at the house he shared with his friends. I asked him if he was going to classes; he said he was but not today because he had no classes on that particular day. When I informed him that the school told me he never showed up for any class after the first day, his only reply was that since this was a private matter between him and the school, there was no way I could be sure. It felt like a sledgehammer hit me in the chest. I flew back to America the next week really disappointed in my son. What more can I say.

Back in North Carolina, we moved into a twelve-thousand-square-foot building in Blue Ridge. Buying antiques for this big building was going to be fun! We went to England in April of 1996 to hand pick a container for the new venture. I met John Payne of Payne's Glass Trading in the backyard of a pub close to Nottingham. John had two thousand windows stacked in piles of twenty. We negotiated a price of five pounds each for a total price of ten thousand pounds or fifteen thousand dollars. Nikki was not too sure this amount of windows would sell in a small place in northern Georgia. Anyway we both thought that maybe this was not so good, but the deal was done and we had to get on with it at this point.

The new sea freight container arrived in Blue Ridge at the end of May just in time for the start of tourist season and summer lake holidays. That first summer, we sold one hundred windows a week for forty dollars each. This was just crazy, and wonderful! Nikki was absolutely right about moving to the Blue Ridge Mountains. Business that year was great, and we were packing containers now out of the Grantham area in England.

We made lots of friends in Blue Ridge after opening the warehouse. Nikki attended the Episcopal Church in Hayesville, where she would drag me on some Sundays with a promise of breakfast at Tommy's, who was known for his biscuits and homemade gravy. Nikki went to services in the Blue Ridge Episcopal Church, St. Luke's, and Rector Victor Morgan was a regular in the antique shop, especially as he was a true anglophile pining for one of his many trips to the old country. Victor liked to visit Nikki and listen to her posh English school accent. When Nikki wasn't able to be in the warehouse or we were on a buying trip to England, our good friends Martha Kay, Bob and Betty, Tom and Cynthia, or Keith and Lois Simpson would help out. Keith was a renowned artist from England now living in Blairsville.

Our dinner parties were large; sometimes as many as fourteen people would gather around our ten-foot antique plank table we got from one of our trips to Hungary. These parties would also happen at other houses on the lake, all summer long, at least once a week. Donna, Laurie, Nikki's cousin, and their son, Bill, came over from Suffolk County on the east coast of England several times in the early 1990s. Once, Donna swam across the lake and back, covering about two miles! They mixed in very well with Nikki's newfound friends. Nikki was like a sister to her lovely cousins. She was so outgoing and loved by all who crossed her path.

After opening the new warehouse in May 1996, we sold lots of merchandise during the grand-opening weekend, and we both had to get in gear to go back to England in June. We needed to be there for Julliet's graduation from Newcastle University. There we met her boyfriend, a fellow student and ex-naval officer, Dominic King. Nikki, like me, found Dom to be a very polite, a young British gentleman. Julliet graduated with honors in science. We were so proud of her. Jonathan was with us, still attending Aberdeen University. We all stayed in Whitley Bay that week with lots of celebrations with Julliet and Dom's friends from school.

The next week we all headed down to Swinderby, Lincolnshire, for the giant antiques fair that they held every two months. The antique dealers arrived with their goods from all over Europe. They came in very large moving vans right down to small panel vans. Some were even in cars pulling their little caravans. Over three thousand dealers set up, and Nikki was in seventh heaven being able to shop until she dropped. She would want to go back to this Swinderby fair every time, even though the December fair was so cold and damp.

After Nikki was through looking at every pitch, we got back to our room at the Brownlow Arms at Hough on the Hill, where we took a hot bath then went down to the bar for five o'clock drinks. Loraine and Paul owned the inn. They were dealers we looked after for many years, packing their goods in our containers for pick up in Blue Ridge, Georgia, and they would meet us in the lounge. There were large, overstuffed armchairs and couches, which were a welcome sight right in front of the log-burning fireplace. We had so much fun with all of the dealers we knew. Nikki, of course, was the lady to see if they needed extra funds or their bookings and transport or rental vehicles.

Pier Farouk was always in residence, with his Poirot accent and looks, a very colorful fellow. His wife, Loraine, was always friendly and also very helpful. Every time we visited their tent at the other large fair we went to, she would offer a coffee or lunch. Loraine and Paul, the innkeepers, would arrange tables in the dining room so we could all discuss the days experiences or life in general. Nikki would sometimes travel to these venues with our daughter, Julliet, or her good friend Jimetta while Jonathan, our son, would arrange container packing or picking up on the fair grounds.

These trips were all the same in 1997, except for a few buying trips to Hungary. We were all so busy that year. Steve Rothrock wanted us to send containers into Georgetown, South Carolina, to set up to sell in a two-week period, only to antique dealers. This was a lot of hard work. Wayne Shockley helped us set up, and he was also a good salesman. Cham and Connie were our best customers, and we became very good friends. Steve had a guesthouse in McClellanville where we had stayed before about thirty minutes south of Charleston, South Carolina close to his house on the sound. We would stay in the guesthouse with our dog, Napier. The goods that were leftover would be taken to the Blue Ridge warehouse and shop.

Nikki would still commute with me and sometimes go on her own to take care of a client's container along with ours. Jonathan, our son, loaded the containers as well as chauffeuring Nikki and our clients to antique shops and fairs. About this time we met and became friends with Will Sergeant and Clare Plumber. They would show up with a picnic basket and wine while we were loading containers. Nikki and I loved their cooking and their companionship.

For something like 15 years, Nikki made sure to include an extra week for staying and visiting with friends and relatives during her five trips a year to the UK.

Before we knew it, it was time to go and winter in Florida. It was nice to see George Geier again on the island;

Napier was my only companion on that journey. We had dropped Nikki off at the Atlanta Airport to go do the antique fairs in England with Julliet. Napier could not wait to be on the island again; he especially loved it in the golf cart. That first night she slept in the cart until three a.m.— what a dog! The next day I started unpacking. Nikki wanted everything done before she arrived in the next ten days. She did not like to cross over the bay because of her fear of boats, so this meant the shopping for four months was down to me, as usual. Nikki made this clear from the first winter onward. I did not mind; I loved this old part of Florida, like you would love a sweetheart.

Nikki arrived in Tampa at Lee and Jimetta's the next day. She got in too late to make the crossing in the dark, so I drove to Tampa, anxiously traveling with our dog, Napier. I could not wait to see Nikki and have her company on this secluded island again! As always, we had many visitors and dinner parties. This particular year, my brother Fred and his family came.

April came quickly, and it was time to go back to our Lake Nottely home. It was also nice to get back to Blairsville, on McIntosh Road and back to the antique warehouse. Nikki got a phone call from Julliet saying that she and Dom were going to get married. Now, everything else was put on the back burner. We had a dinner party in the beginning of May where Nikki told everyone about the wedding. It was to be held on September 11, 1998, in England.

Nikki had chosen Lumley Castle in Durham for the dinner and dance. Whitley Bay Church of England was for the service, and all of the ladies were to wear hats while the men were to wear gray top hats and tails. Since custom has it that the parents of the bride have to pay for the wedding, wherever it was going to be, that's what we did. Nikki never did discuss any costs with me or say how much everything would be for 125 meals in the guest hall. There would be a choice of either beef or lamb, champagne to toast, and a choice of wines that were to flow during the meal and the speeches. Dom's brother's speech lasted almost an hour. My speech was only three minutes, thank God! Some of the guests even went to lie down between finishing up the meal and waiting for the first dance. Jonathan was now living in Grantham with his girlfriend, Alison, who looked lovely, as did Julliet and Nikki. Dom and Jonathan looked very handsome in their wedding gear.

We asked one of our good friends, Meredith to do the video taping of the complete festivities plus videoing Julliet getting ready along with her bridesmaids. Since this was to be a personal matter, we wanted Meredith and not some stranger to go into their rooms. Nikki asked all of the Americans that were flying over to bring two bottles of champagne with them. When the wedding ceremony was over at the church, we had to travel for ninety minutes from Whitley Bay to near Durham Cathedral where Lumley Castle was. When we all came out of the church, a large group of people wanted to know who was getting married. They were all looking over a four-foot wall since there were so many men in top hats and tails. All the ladies wore beautiful wide-brim hats as well.

There was a Rolls Royce for Julliet and Dom and Nikki and me, but when Nikki saw an iced-down case of champagne go on to the large tour bus, she took my hand and said, "We are going on the bus!" Before the bus was on the move, two cases of champagne glasses were opened, and the bottles were being popped. The bus ran into heavy traffic on the way up, but we didn't mind since we all were sipping champagne. Our driver was good, and he got Nikki to the castle before the wedding car and many others. Nikki looked grand greeting the guests. Julliet was stunning, a very beautiful bride.

This was some week. Before the day of the wedding, Nikki and I, along with twenty others, had stayed at the Marquis Hotel on the sea front and partied hard for five nights. Now the wedding was another big party. Liam, Dom's brother, came up to me at the end of the night and said, "When you Americans throw a party, you *really* throw a party!"

Nikki and I were getting ready to go back to Lake Nottely in a few days. I was looking forward to a rest. A group of us traveled together, and two days later we were at Jacque and David's house in Hathersage before flying out of Manchester. Julliet and Dom were headed to the Caribbean for their honeymoon. We made it back to the lake in Georgia, and one week later a hurricane came barreling down on the island where Julliet and Dom were. They flew back to Atlanta then drove to the lake to stay with us. We relived the wedding over and over; it was so good to see them. They flew back to England the next week.

Nikki and I were packing up to go to Little Gasparilla Island in four weeks. We think the dog knew—she was extra bouncy. It always took a long time to get to our island gear ready. Of course, Nikki had to call everyone she knew in England, Scotland, Canada, and America to let them know where we could be reached, giving them the island phone number. Nikki also had to finish up the tax returns and give banking instructions to the accountant and our warehouse manager.

At the beginning of November, and we were back on the island. Everyone knew we were back, and from the next day on, friends started dropping by at five o'clock for the sunsets. Most of the time we would congregate on George Geier's deck to watch the sunset, and we would all bring a snack along. We left early that year, at the end of February. The red tide was too much for us, and dead fish washed ashore daily, hundreds of them. Nikki said the winter was almost over anyway and we needed to pack up and head back up to the lake. We could not believe that 1999 was here already. It felt good in a way to be back in time to see the dogwood trees bloom.

Chapter 11

Together Again

Ro's Story

Christmas of 1985 we were all together, and I knew Geoff and Di and Granny were very happy to have the family back. For New Year's, John and I stayed at the Sylvia Hotel by Stanley Park in Vancouver. In the morning, we watched the polar-bear swim. During those two days, John told me all about the affair and asked me to never let "her" know that I knew. I promised him I would not. There were occasions when that certain lady and I were together over the next few years, but I always kept my word.

Only my friends at work knew about the separation. Linda was very supportive and helped me a lot. For the first time in my life I didn't confide in Nikki. I am not sure why; maybe it would have made it too real or I was simply in denial. When everything was back on track, I told her all about it, and she understood as always. Lloyd and Nikki were very relieved that their friends were a couple again.

John and I were dating again; we loved meeting after work for a glass of wine and an appetizer and staying overnight at one of our homes. We were busy making plans for the future and knew we could not go back to how it was in the house on Seventy-sixth Avenue. We put the house on the market, and I gave notice at the townhouse. Maybe the answer was to get an apartment in town for three of the girls. Tanya and Gary, who were less mature, would live with us in a new house.

We found a really nice house at the right price on Forty-ninth Avenue in Langley; both of us loved it the moment we walked in. Sharon and Joanne thought the apartment was a great idea and so we got one for them in town, close to the shops and the bus stop. But Cara said she would rather live with the Brett family, as Mike Brett was her boyfriend, and somehow we agreed.

Northwest Digital was once again doing well and providing us with a good income. John's tests came back negative so an ulcer was ruled out. Further tests were needed. Many weeks went by with no diagnosis. We were beginning to enjoy a less-stressful life with just two kids and one dog when, after only a month in our new home, John was told he had a malignant tumor in his bowel. It was devastating news, and we were very scared. But at the same time we were also hopeful that after the operation, he would have a full recovery and we'd have our life back. We kept optimistic for each other. I called Nikki in Scotland, and she and Lloyd were very shocked at the news. I knew they would be praying for us. In England Daphne and Alan, Pauline and Cris, Lyn and Pete, and all of our other friends were wonderful in their caring and support. Geoff and Di were extremely upset, of course. Thank goodness they lived close by; I was so grateful for their help over the next couple of years.

I took a leave of absence from work; the kids, of course, were traumatised. I can't pretend to know what went on their heads; it must have been tough. They had school and they had their friends, thank goodness. Sharon and Jo were at the apartment most of the time, and there wasn't too much communication. Cara came over quite a bit, and her support was much appreciated.

John had the operation, and I remember as he came around in the recovery room, he was screaming in pain. I rushed to the nurses' station for them to give him something, but they told me it was too soon for more medication. I was hysterical, not knowing how to help him. Later, when he was fully conscious, he couldn't remember any of it—what a blessing that was! A few days later, he was sitting on the side of the bed with his head hanging down, and he said to me, "This is far from being over; I have to have chemotherapy when I'm strong enough, and still the cancer could come back."

John came home and slowly improved. The chemo we administered at home, but halfway through, he said no more, it made him feel too ill. I'll never know how that decision affected the final outcome. We had wonderful support from everyone and were very grateful for it every day.

My mum and dad were in the process of immigrating to Canada. Poor Dad was to suffer years of paperwork battles with the government, but he was determined to come over and live close to us. Mum had the start of Alzheimer's symptoms years before, but we hoped we could get her over here anyway—probably foolishly, looking back now. With John being sick, though, they felt the need to be over here even more. The plan was for them to sell their maisonette in Rickmansworth, Hertfordshire, and then I would go over and get Mum and bring her to Canada. Dad would sell last-minute stuff, tie up all the loose ends, and follow.

John was recovering well. I can remember the day he put on his suit to go into work, looked in the mirror, and said, "Not bad for someone who's just recovered from cancer." I told him how great he looked, and he did. I went back to work at Raymond's, casually as a floater, just filling in where I was needed in several lower mainland locations. It was good to get back to the outside world. I believe we had a year of relatively normal life—if you can with five seventeen-year-olds! There was a whole lot of trouble at the apartment. It had, of course, become a party place, and all sort of odd bodies were sleeping there at different times. John and I even made a surprise visit in the middle of the night, and it just confirmed our suspicions. That was the end of it. Sharon went to stay with Geoff and Di, and Joanne came home. That was as angry as I'd ever seen John with the kids. But I think they still thought it was my idea to surpise them and get them in trouble.

The next thing was for me to go and get Mum. That flight back with her was quite something, and I was so worried about what she would say to the customs officer. I had tried to coach her, but her mind came and went and I couldn't be sure what would happen. Some greater power was on my side, and somehow we got through—and there were John and Geoff waiting for us at the airport—such a relief!

We had Mum with us for a few weeks before Dad arrived. She wasn't sure where she was half the time, which was probably a blessing. She loved seeing the kids; they were very kind and patient with her. I had to be home with her the rest of the time because she couldn't be left alone. When Dad arrived, he soon found a house not too far away, a small rancher, and from then on, he looked after Mum.

John was feeling very well so we planned a holiday in Maui for two weeks in early December 1986. It was absolutely the best time we'd had in years; every day was magical. We enjoyed each moment from walking and swimming on the beach to shrimp lunches and fish dinners overlooking the water. That lovely, warm evening air, the sunsets—we wanted to live there because we loved it so much. Of course, we came back to Langley and had a family Christmas. Little did we know that it would be our last.

Early in January 1987, John had a routine checkup at the cancer clinic in Vancouver. We went back to check the results. The doctor did not even take him into a private room. They just stood in the hallway, and I was sitting in the waiting area. I could see the color drain from John's face when they told him that the cancer was back. My heart sank. We went for a walk in Stanley Park and decided to be optimistic and fight this awful disease. We really encouraged each other and felt a lot better by the time we got home.

Everyone at Northwest Digital was very supportive, and John just worked at home from then on. Janice, his PA, went to work looking for alternative treatments and clinics all over the States and Mexico. We had to tell the kids, of course, our parents, and all of our friends. Everyone was dismayed; everyone loved John. Why would this happen to him? Janice came up with a clinic in San Diego that had had some amazing successes. In fact, several of the doctors there were cancer survivors themselves. It was expensive but sounded like the best chance of beating the cancer without chemo or radiation. The doctor told us that another operation was not an option.

It was the third week in February when we flew to San Diego and checked into the Livingston Wheeler Clinic. In the reception area there was a file of all patients who had been cured. It made a good impression, and we felt really optimistic. At this point you could not tell which one of us was the patient.

During the next two weeks, we went there Monday through Friday for about six hours a day. John had lots of tests, and we had nutrition classes and instruction on what we had to do and what to eat. John was prescribed a lot of vitamins and minerals, some daily injections, and coffee enemas.

On the weekend he bought a new set of Ping golf clubs, and I caddied for him as he played Torrey Pines. It was a glorious day, probably the last we had to enjoy. We came home armed with bottles of vitamins, minerals, and the dreaded liver powder, which had to be mixed in carrot juice and drunk—ugh!

Dad had been minding the house, kids, and dog with Mum in tow and was waiting with a meal ready. John, on his own restricted diet, couldn't eat most of it unfortunately. For one moment, I can remember thinking selfishly, *How am I going to deal with all of this?* But it went in a flash and never came back. John was in the fight of his life, and nothing would be too much trouble for me to do for him.

We got a Champion juicer, and I juiced five pounds of carrots a day. There was no meat or fish for three months. Then we could look forward to New Zealand lamb, because it was grass fed with no chemicals, and certain kinds of tuna. The eggs from vaccinated chickens we had shipped from San Diego, and only a few were ever broken. The diet involved lots of raw vegetables, rice, beans, nuts, and seeds. We had a recipe book, and I made nut loaves and fake macaroni and cheese. John was in some pain at this stage, so he was allowed Advil. He was slowly looking weaker. In April, he had a bad turn and was rushed to

Surrey Memorial Hospital. They relieved the pain, took X-rays, etc. I remember the doctor who told me that the cancer was spreading and there was basically no hope.

John and I stayed together in that hospital for a month; they gave me a small bed next to his, and we had our own bathroom. I went home every day or so to check on things, change clothes, etc. Dad had Woody, the dog, and the kids managed to look after themselves. While he was in the hospital, John started an outline for a book he wanted to write about our lives, but he never got the time to start it. He asked his doctor at the hospital to call the doctor at the Livingston Wheeler Clinic to see if they could work together for his benefit, but he wouldn't—understandable, I suppose.

There was awful day when John had a fit and I thought I'd lost him! I was screaming and crying, absolutely beside myself. The doctors and nurses rushed in and somehow brought him back. I'm glad that it never happened again. We went home in the middle of May and celebrated his forty-third birthday on the twenty-sixth.

John was hoping to have a tuna sandwich, but he couldn't eat it; and it was getting more and more difficult to get all of the pills down. The only thing he could manage to drink was the pear juice from a can of fruit. So for weeks I was giving everyone pears with no juice.

There came a point where he could not eat solid food at all and was on Ensure. He could only handle the vanilla flavor. I stayed home the whole time apart from going to the corner store on occasion. I was on tender hooks all the time because of leaving him alone, even if I was only ten minutes. We had a home-care nurse come in once a day, and soon she was dressing a horrible bed sore at the base of his spine. She told me it would never heal; that really shook me up! Now he had to have morphine for the pain, and I was instructed how to do the injections. He was still managing to get out of bed in the middle of the day. I'd help him onto the chaise lounge, and he'd lie with this eyes closed and breathe the fresh air. One day, I saw him look at himself in the mirror and realize he was looking at a dying man. It was so incredibly sad. I'll never forget it.

John's brother Geoff and his wife, Di, were very supportive, as were John's mum and my dad. His oldest brother, Peter, came to visit him from Portland, Oregon, and his partner from work, Rob, came rolling up in his sports car one day while John was resting outside. John told me afterwards that although it was nice to see him, the contrast in their situations was too evident to him; Rob, handsome and full of life and energy, talking about work; and John, struggling to even talk and looking and feeling so ill.

Nikki was often calling me to give me love and support. She and Lloyd were very busy in their antiques business at the time, and it made traveling up to B.C. impossible. Anyway John was getting to the point that he didn't want visitors except the kids and close family. Even that was a strain; the pain was increasing and hope was decreasing. John needed morphine injections every three or four hours, and he needed me to be there all the time. Nursing him was not a hard thing to do; he never complained or demanded anything, and he was so incredibly brave. Every moment at this point we treasured; we were in a kind of cocoon and as close as two people can get.

Our twenty-first anniversary was on September 17, and how John managed to have flowers delivered without me knowing, I'll never know. It more than made up for that awful day three years earlier. It got to the stage where John could no longer get out of bed; the bedsore was horrendous, and the morphine was increased. He existed on a little pear juice and Ensure and was sleeping more and more.

Friday, November 13, we were in bed; *Dallas* was on the TV then *Falcon Crest*, which had just started when Cara arrived. We were discussing why she was so late when Cara looked at John and said, "Mum, I think Dad has died." She was right. John was dead. It was unbelievable and shocking that he was gone forever from this world, even though we knew it was inevitable. The doctor was called, and by the time he signed the death certificate it was past midnight, so it was dated November 14, 1987. John was taken away in a body bag, an image that will never go away. The next days were a blur. The kids told me that the bedroom door was locked for hours.

Janice from Northwest Digital stepped right in and organized the funeral. It was probably a good thing. She was very efficient, and there was the coffin to choose and the burial site. There were a lot of decisions to be made at a very difficult time. Geoff went with me, and we settled on Valley View in Surrey. They talked me into a double plot with our names engraved and the dates, one, of course yet to be completed. There was a big turnout for the funeral. So many wonderful things said; he was loved by so many people. How very sad for his mother and my parents, who loved him so much and five seventeen-year-olds whom he loved so dearly and were now without their dad.

Woody, our pet cockapoo, came back home from Mum and Dad's and I started going for very long walks twice a day. I spent a lot of time putting together a small album for each of the children with pictures of John and personal photos of them with their dad. There was a lot of paperwork to deal with: lawyers, accountants, vehicle transfers; it was all very new to me. I was getting used to paying the bills, which before John got sick I had never done.

John left Lloyd his cardinal watch. Lloyd was very moved when he heard. I stupidly wore it one day soon after the death, to have something of John's close to me, and I promptly lost it. It fell off my wrist, being so big. I was very upset, but Lloyd understood. He said that it was the thought that John had remembered him in his will, and that he had evidently treasured their friendship, which mattered.

That first Christmas was terrible for us all. There were invitations, but I was not anywhere near ready to face the world without John. The children must have been suffering, too. Counseling had been offered to them, but no one wanted it. I guess we all felt we could cope without it and were not ready to talk.

Unfortunately, John's death did not bring the family closer together. In fact, it did the opposite, and although Cara was still supportive and caring, quite a rift developed between me and Sharon, Joanne, Tanya, and Gary. Thank goodness today we have all forgiven and moved on to loving and caring about one another.

My poor dad was struggling. He'd just lost his beloved son-in-law and taken on a lot of responsibility with the children; and now my mum's Alzheimer's was getting worse. She'd also fallen and broken her hand and was becoming very tearful. They had no medical insurance so that was an added worry.

Even though Dad needed my help with Mum at home, I applied for a job as a home-care worker. The wages were very low, but I wanted to give something back to the organization that had helped John and me so much. It was a crazy thing to do when my own parents needed my help. I do believe that I was not thinking rationally at that time about anything. I found the job very hard physically and emotionally, so after a few months, I quit. Dad had, in the meantime, gotten some paid help in, and luckily it worked out quite well. Now I had time to support Mum and Dad the best I could.

The house now needed some attention, and it was also something to occupy my mind. The roof needed replacing, and so I got that done, even though it seemed an awful lot of money to me! The rooms upstairs in the house also needed painting so I called a painter we had used in the past, Robert. He came over to give me an estimate. He was very sorry that John had died and gave me a very good deal. I was beginning to know prices a bit by now. He started the work a week later. Robert was very kind to me, and I really needed a friend right then. I even helped him remove the wallpaper in the bathroom, just for the company. In the end there was nothing left to be painted in the house; he'd even painted the carport. Finally after weeks of painting, he packed up his stuff and left, telling me to call him if there were any touch-ups needed. A couple of weeks later, I discovered a number of places that did indeed need touching up, so I called him back. That was the beginning of a tumultuous relationship that somehow lasted nineteen years.

Robert was as opposite from John as one could imagine, and so, naturally, no one thought he was right for me. My dad, as always, was very kind and understanding but I think all of the kids thought I was crazy. Robert took me out to eat, and we went for a few trips over the border twenty miles away, to the States for social events and shopping. We'd also go to local fairs and car shows with his 1960s Lincoln town car. It was good to have some fun again. Robert helped me a lot with the yard and cut the grass, which I appreciated. He was estranged from his second wife at that time and was planning to divorce. A few months later, he moved in.

Meanwhile, Mum was getting worse, and it was heartbreaking to see her in such a state. Dad was so patient and kind with her; he was not a strong man anymore but managed to get her in and out of the bed and into the bathroom. It was ten months after John's death when I got a call that Mum had died. I rushed to the house, and Dad was weeping and saying that he had lost his sweetheart. It turned out that she had been suffering from lung cancer too, but she had been unable to tell us what she was feeling so it was never discovered while she was alive. Dad wanted me to speak at the funeral and with his help to write the eulogy. Robert was there, and it was a fairly strained situation. At least poor Mum was at peace now—no more crying.

Since I had shared this house with John, Robert did not feel very comfortable living in it, understandably, I suppose. Therefore with his encouragement, I put the house up for sale. I must have had it priced too low because it sold very quickly, and then I was under pressure to find somewhere else to live. Robert took me looking in earnest, and it was extremely stressful. There was not a lot on the market at that time so choices were limited. With little time to spare I settled on a house that was only a few miles away on a nice cul-de-sac. It had a big room off of the kitchen, which Robert liked because he wanted us to get a pool table. We moved into the house together, and I soon bought a big, beautiful pool table. We had Dad over quite a bit to play pool. He was a very good player and enjoyed teaching me.

Dad was forced, financially, to sell his house, and we thought it would be fine if he had a small RV on our lot because we had lots of room. Robert and Dad got on quite well, and I thought it could work. I wanted to help Dad and for him to be happy. It did work for a while, but one day after the neighbor's dog peed on our front step, Robert went over to complain, and he happened to have a hammer in his hand as he had been fixing something. Naturally enough, the lady took it as a threat, and in retaliation, she phoned the town council and complained about Dad's motor home. We soon had a bylaw officer at the house telling us it had to go. The only solution was to move somewhere that had a basement suite for Dad. The five kids, who were nineteen now, were living in various rental accommodations, either sharing with friends or each other. For a number of years they all had a history of moving every few months. My dad, Granny Letts, and Uncle Geoff and Auntie Di were steadying influences in their lives; thank goodness because only Cara had any communication with me.

We had to go as far down the Trans-Canada Highway as Abbotsford to find a house with a basement suite in my price range. The only trouble was that it had an in-ground pool, which was expensive to keep and we hardly used it. Robert couldn't swim. It did have room for the pool table, which had become important to us.

Soon after Robert and I started living together, I began helping him with his painting business. I quite enjoyed it, but sometimes he was a hard taskmaster. On one occasion we painted an old house in Langley that belonged to a seventy-eight-year-old lady called Queen. She was very sweet and kind and always asking us in for tea. We thought it might be nice for my dad to meet her. They got on well together. She was a good cook, and Dad had a car and could drive her about, so it worked very well.

Northwest Digital looked like it was going to be taken over by The Harco Corporation and that would mean about five hundred thousand dollars for my shares. This was pretty exciting, and so Robert and I planned a motoring trip in the States for about seven weeks, stopping in Las Vegas to get married. I did not feel any pressing need to marry, but Robert was extremely keen on it and I thought Las Vegas sounded exciting. My lawyer advised me to get a prenuptial agreement drawn up. Robert thought it unnecessary but reluctantly signed it. About a week before the deadline, Harco backed out of the deal; it was a nasty shock but we carried on with the plans to go on the trip. Dad said he would look after the house and Woody, my dog; and now he had Queen for company.

Robert and I got married at the Candlelight Chapel—the first one we came to—on January 12, 1990. Just a little farther down the road was Graceland Chapel, and Robert, being a huge Elvis fan, would have loved that. Our plan was to drive down to Florida, where I would introduce Robert to Nikki and Lloyd. Meanwhile, Cara had broken up with her boyfriend, Mike, and was visiting Nikki, Lloyd, and Julliet, who was just a year younger than Cara.

We took about three weeks to get there, driving a lot of back roads and staying at cheap motels. It was a lot of fun. I loved seeing Nikki again and their house on the golf course. Unfortunately, Nikki did not care for Robert, and that opinion would never change. Lloyd was very busy in real estate at the time so we didn't see that much of him. Robert and I took Cara and Julliet to Disney World and the Epcot Center, which was fantastic; and after a couple more days, we started our long drive home.

When we got back to Abbotsford, Dad told us he had asked Queen to marry him. It was wonderful to see him so happy, especially after nursing Mum all that time. Unfortunately it was looking like his bladder cancer might be back. He was scheduled for some tests, and if he needed treatment, Queen would look after him. When you are in your late seventies, there is no time to waste, so the wedding was to be March 10. It was a very nice wedding, and Dad and Queen were extremely happy. They lived in Queen's little house that Robert and I had painted.

Robert put his ad back in the paper and managed to get some painting work, but now the house was too large for us and the pool was a constant problem—so up it went for sale and we were on the move again! This time we ended up in Sardis, a few more miles east down the Trans-Canada Highway. We found an old ranch house on an acre, and I made the huge mistake of putting it in joint names, not realizing that would pretty well cancel out the prenuptial agreement. I spent a lot of my money on that house. The chicken barn outside was converted into a Western theme cowboy bar with a pool table and a separate bathroom. The whole place needed updating, and we had a lovely new oak kitchen put in. All the wiring had to be upgraded, as did the plumbing. Robert, of course, did all the painting.

Now that we were out in the country, we thought we needed a guard dog, so off we went to the SPCA. Robert wanted a male shepherd cross, but we went home with a female Husky. We thought she was male at first and called her Sheriff. She and her sibling had been found in a box at the side of a busy highway, and although she was a lovely, sweet dog, she never learned to play and she was not a very good guard dog. So off we went to SPCA again and came back with Marshall.

He was a lab/shepherd cross, definitely male, big and black; and he was going to sleep outside and be a guard dog. That was Robert's plan, but Marshall never spent one night outside of the house. We had all three dogs—Woody, Sheriff, and Marshall—sleep in the laundry room with their own beds. Tootsie, the cat, would sleep anywhere she chose.

Spending all of this money was a great concern to me. Robert's painting was very up and down, so I put in an application with Sears that was only a ten-minute drive from home. They were not taking on new staff at that time, but several months later they called me back for an interview. I was to work there in Lingerie and Ladies Fashions for ten years. I met some wonderful people there and still treasure their friendships, Linda French and Irma Hovik in particular. They saw me through some very rough times with Robert.

My uncle Peter, my dad's only brother, was 64 and traveling in Germany, when suddenly he dropped dead from a heart attack. Dad and Queen went over to England to sort everything out. He had been living alone in a maisonette in Watford, and the place was an absolute disaster. The backyard was completely overgrown; no one could walk out there at all. The inside was in such a mess it was hard to believe he could actually have been living there.

However, he was still working for a big insurance company and had a good life insurance policy which, because he died before sixty-five, was a large sum. There was no will, but Dad was his closest relative so it all went to him. My dad really deserved this; he'd been a very generous man all of his life and very hardworking. He always had just enough money but not much extra, so this apart from the sadness of it, was wonderful!

Dad gave a big lump sum to the Christadelphian Church, which Peter belonged to, and he gave away lots to all the family. Now they could sell Queen's small house and get something better, which they did. How Dad enjoyed the freedom to buy a nice home and have new furniture. He really enjoyed life with Queen. Unfortunately his health was breaking down a bit, but it did not stop them from driving across Canada and back. It amazed us all, but it was the trip of a lifetime for them. All good things come to an end, and Dad's health worsened. He was feeling sick a lot of the time and was eating less and less. Again, the diagnosis was slow in coming, but when it did it was bad. It was cancer of the esophagus. There was briefly some talk of operating, but he wasn't strong enough to even go through the preparations.

I remember the doctor seemed a very cold man without any bedside manner or kindness toward my dad. But we were at his mercy so I said nothing. I had only been at Sears for two weeks, but they told me to take as much time off as I needed.

So I drove every day from Sardis to New Westminster, which took well over an hour, and visited Dad; we had some lovely talks. He was still reading, learning, and interested in new things right to the end. He had started writing a book about politics, and I was sorry I couldn't carry on his dream of getting it finished.

Dad died a couple of weeks later in my arms. I miss him still today as much as ever, and he will never be forgotten by anyone who ever knew him. The day of the funeral, I managed to stand up (this time without his help) and tell everyone what a great father he was, but of course, everyone already knew this. He was not at all ready to die, that's for sure. He had an incredible zest for life, and there was still so much he wanted to do. Dad's Queen, of course, had her new life suddenly cut short, but at least she had enjoyed two happy years with him. My kids were wonderful; they made all the sandwiches and prepared the food for the wake, which was held at Queen's and Dad's home. For some reason, two of Robert's brothers turned up with girlfriends in tow and made inroads into the food like gannets. They were not at the service and in fact hardly knew Dad. One of them even made a pass at my daughter, Sharon. It took me years to finally forgive them.

I missed my dad terribly and still do today, but I know he's one of my guardian angels and is still looking after me.

Queen was now alone in that big house. For a while, she had Tanya and Gary staying with her plus an elderly friend called Verna, but of course, she soon decided to sell. The majority of the money to buy the house had come from Dad, and now it all belonged to Queen including all of the brand-new furniture. Just before Dad died, he and Queen made new wills, and apart from a small lump sum for the five kids and me, everything went to Queen while she lived. She had no children, so in her will, a certain percentage was to go to her first husband's niece. Dad was adamant that her side of the family (through her first husband) would not suffer financially because of their marriage. The bulk of the estate, which came from my dad and my uncle Peter and whatever was left, should come to our family, me and the kids.

Queen's niece soon caught on to this, and it was not long after Dad's death that she got Queen to change her will, which legally she had every right to do. Morally it was letting my dad down big time. Queen bought a small town house where she lived with Verna for about five years before they had to go into a nursing home. Her mind was gradually going before that; she nearly sold her house to her hairdresser for one thousand dollars, but thankfully her niece was able to stop that and promptly got power of attorney.

The end result was that Queen's first husband's niece got the bulk of my dad's and uncle's estates and there was nothing I could do about it. I did go to a lawyer, but Dad had foolishly trusted Queen to not change her will and did not take into account that she could and would be persuaded to do it. Our family visited Queen during her last five years. We were all fond of her and wanted to stay in contact for Dad's sake. Tanya and Gary often stayed there, and they always got free rent, which the niece did not like, and she might have been right about that.

In 1994, Cara was working in Banff, Alberta, as a waitress and making very good money. While she was there she met and fell in love with a handsome barman named Stephen Baird. He was a few years older than her, and she was swept off of her feet. With her brother and sisters all attending, they got married in the hotel where Stephen worked. It is of great sadness to me that I did not know about the wedding until after it was all over.

Back in Sardis I was enjoying my job at Sears, but Robert was struggling with his painting work. There was just not enough money coming in. He persuaded me to think of selling our house and buying a smaller, cheaper place closer to town and getting a mortgage to buy a small apartment block so that he could be a landlord. I was too easily persuaded because I knew instinctively that it would be a mistake. However, I went along with it, and by 1993, we owned, along with the bank, a block of seven apartments with a one-bedroom in the middle, then two units with two bedrooms on each side, and a three-bedroom on each end. They were all relatively small with no yards, but we built lockers in the back for storage.

It was nine years of total stress! Robert did not have the right temperament to be a landlord, and the only renters we could get were people who were subsidized by the government—and most of them, I'm afraid to say, had no respect for other peoples' property. Many times, they would skip out with no notice, leaving an awful mess behind. I remember one time there were eggs thrown on every wall and holes kicked in every door. Financially it was a strain, sometimes having to put the mortgage payment on a credit card. One day, one of the tenants, a heavy woman, was walking from the laundry room to her apartment. It was raining, and she was wearing flip-flops and carrying the laundry. She slipped and fell. Robert happened to be there and was not very sympathetic, so she ended up suing us and got ten thousand dollars. Luckily we were insured and only had to pay the deductible of five hundred.

In 1995, all of the grief and bitterness over John's death was dissolving and all of the scars were gradually fading. I felt I had to be the one to start mending fences. Robert was supportive in this, and so we planned a family barbeque inviting all five kids, Granny Letts, and Geoff and Di. It was a lovely summer day and everyone came.

Robert burned the chicken but nobody minded. It really was a turning point for the family. I didn't know that day, but Sharon was pregnant and it was so wonderful to feel I had my daughter back!

Although my family would not have chosen Robert for me, they began to accept him for what he was, and he helped them physically, many times. He had a big cube van, and it seemed like every other month one of them was moving; but he never shied away when they needed help.

It was now 1996. The night Sharon went into labor I was at home alone because Robert had stormed out of the house earlier in the afternoon in a fit of temper over a financial disagreement with me. She was in St. Paul's Hospital in Vancouver. I had no idea how to get there and it was about six p.m. I got into my car and drove, full of anticipation, up Highway 1 into Vancouver. I took the First Avenue exit, hoping it was right, and stopped at various gas stations to ask the way. Miraculously, I'm not sure how, I finally got there. Sharon's friend Jennifer was already there, and between us we helped Sharon get through the next few hours of labor. She wanted me there at the birth, which meant so much to me, and the most beautiful little girl was born in the early hours of June 26, 1996. Sharon named her Crimson, and that beautiful baby has grown into an even more beautiful young woman. Robert did show up and was very humble toward me for his behavior the previous evening. He was taken aback by how lovely Sharon and her baby were.

When Crimson was a few months old, Sharon let me, Robert, and Joanne take her to Alberta to introduce her to Cara and Stephen, and I think to give her a break. It was a lovely trip, and we all got on very well. Later that year, Sharon and her long-time boyfriend, Darin Edwards, decided to get married. They wanted the ceremony to be up Cypress Mountain on December 2. They have always liked the unconventional! This time Robert and I were invited, and I gave them my wedding ring from John, hoping they would be as happy as her father and I had been. Robert gave Sharon away, and despite shivering she looked beautiful. It was a freezing cold day, but we all warmed up in the pub afterwards.

Sharon, Darin, and Crimson lived for a few years in Chilliwack so I really enjoyed my granddaughter, an easy child with a sweet disposition.

Tanya and Gary stuck together during these years, moving up Revelstoke, British Columbia. Tanya was always interested in singing and writing, and they were both movie fanatics. I didn't see much of them but always heard through the grapevine how they were getting on. Joanne was taking a travel-agent course but soon found it was going to be too stressful for her to work in that industry. Jo is such a kind and caring person, we all thought that nursing would be a good career choice for her, but again in reality, it was too much physically and mentally.

Robert and I were hanging in there, some good days and some not so good. We had our three dogs, Marshall, Sheriff, and poor old Woody, who was nearing the end of his days. All through my life my dogs have given me enormous pleasure, and I especially appreciated them in the tough times. Walking dogs is the best therapy I know. Robert often complained that he lived in a dog's house, which I suppose he did, but he loved them, too, in his way and was always kind to them.

Nikki and Lloyd were living in Georgia at this time. I always looked forward to our weekly phone calls. Their antique business was doing well, and between us there was always so much to talk about. It was sometime in late 1997 that Nikki called to say Julliet was getting married the following September. It sounded very exciting; Nikki was planning to have the reception in Lumley Castle in northern England, and it all sounded wonderful. Of course I said I would come; I think she was relieved when Robert said he'd stay home and look after the dogs.

I took the opportunity of planning an extended visit so that I could stay with Daphne and Alan and Pauline and Cris afterwards. I hadn't been back to England for many years, and I was excited to see everyone again. It was a long and complicated journey to the Marquis Hotel in Whitley Bay where I finally found myself after two planes, a train, and a taxi. Nikki and Lloyd appeared in the hallway—it was so good to see them at last!

We had several days of get-togethers and parties before the wedding day. A lot of the old Harrow group were there, as were friends from America and Nikki's cousins. The wedding ceremony took place in a lovely country church in Whitley Bay. Julliet was a stunning bride in a most beautiful dress, and all the men in the wedding party were very handsome in their top hats and tails. Then we were all bussed to the castle and served champagne en route. The journey was over an hour, but we were having so much fun and Nikki had planned it all so perfectly. She looked magnificent in pale blue with an enormous hat, and after a lovely sit-down meal, the party went on until the early hours.

The day after the wedding, I went with Nikki and Lloyd to Jacque and David Bevan's beautiful house in the Peak District. You could see Hathersage down in the valley surrounded by the Hope Valley. The view reminded me of the village "Whoville" from the children's story *How the Grinch Stole Christmas* by Dr. Seuss. We all spent the night there before I headed south on the train to see my other friends. Nikki and Lloyd were to fly out of Manchester, which was only an hour's drive from the Bevans' house. It was a fantastic trip, and every time I go to England it seems I leave a little bit of my heart there. Back in Canada after the long plane trip, I planned to see my children so I could share my experiences of England and Julliet's wedding.

Cara and Stephen had been married for four years when Cara got pregnant in 1997. She then wanted to move back to B.C. to be closer to her sisters and me. She came from Alberta to stay with us so that I could help her find an apartment. Steven wanted an ocean view, and we managed to find one in White Rock. They got moved in shortly before Jade Louise was born on March 15, 1998. That was the second time I saw a granddaughter of mine brought into the world. John's mother, Doris Letts, was there in the waiting room. It was a joyous occasion for us all!

The following July, Sharon gave birth to her second child, a lovely boy with reddish blonde hair whom they named Xavier. The family was growing. A year after we had moved to Chilliwack, the army base closed. That meant two thousand families leaving town. Immediately property prices fell drastically, and it would take ten years for them to recover. During our nine years in Chilliwack, we lost three dogs: Woody from old age, Sheriff from stomach cancer, and our black lab, Marshall, from an embolism at eight years old—that was a heartbreaker. We gained Ranger, a Doberman cross, and Patsy, a Springer spaniel cross, and also Cody, the golden retriever that nobody wanted. They were all a huge part of my life and gave me immense happiness.

The year 2000 came in quietly for us. We celebrated our tenth anniversary on January 12 without too much celebration. John had always talked about going out on a golf course in 2040 – I often think of that; was he ever cut short!

Tanya and Gary were living in Revelstoke, British Columbia, looking for new opportunities. Gary worked in a car rental business; he was a very good driver and would deliver cars to Calgary and Vancouver. Tanya lived with her boyfriend, Addy, until they split up. I didn't see them very much during that time. They moved back west to

Vancouver Island in 2006 to be closer to the rest of the family again.

The value of our house and the apartments was still down, and we knew things had to change. Robert had a very short fuse when it came to the tenants, and I thought he might end up in serious trouble if things got any worse.

I was at the ten-year mark at Sears, and I'd had enough of fitting bras and selling credit cards, so I looked forward to a change of lifestyle. Robert wanted a motel, but I saw similar problems with that—and he'd have had me washing towels and cleaning rooms all day long. No thank you! That's how we got started thinking about a bar as an alternative; also, Cara's husband, Stephen, had once told us that if we got him a bar, he'd make us nothing but money!

Now, we didn't know him that well, and likewise, he didn't know us; but we thought with his knowledge of food and beverage and my money, we could run a family business. Cara, Stephen, and Jade, who was now four years old, had moved from White Rock (things didn't work out there) and were back in Alberta. Stephen had got a job in Edmonton, but there were problems so he was ready for a new opportunity.

Robert started looking in the investment papers feverishly and was making lots of phone calls. We still didn't have a computer. He came up with a few possibilities, and we set off to Alberta to look at possible enterprises. Price was a big factor, which made this a pretty short list. Nanton was a small redneck town south of Calgary, consisting mainly of bars and antique shops. The old blacksmith shop was now a small bar and was up for sale. It had a lot of character; the building was over one hundred years old, and we were quite taken with it. We came home, talked it over with Stephen and Cara over the phone, and we all thought we should take a chance on it. Somehow I don't think we investigated it quite enough!

We were lucky: our house in Chilliwack sold for what I'd paid for it nine years earlier. A year later, property prices almost doubled because of the impending Winter Olympics. Robert and I never did have any luck that way. I took a big loss on the sale of the apartments, but I was so happy to be rid of them. I sold my 1979 station wagon, which I loved, but we were doubtful it could make it to Alberta. We needed four-wheel drive for the snow we would be dealing with, so I bought a 1997 Chevy Blazer, which would be an ongoing problem for eight years.

There was a window of time before everything was all signed and sealed, and it just so happened that Nikki and Lloyd were going to be in Las Vegas for a wedding. Nikki called me up to see if we could possibly get down there to meet them. That was too tempting to pass up, and it would be a wonderful break before the big move; plus we had our new vehicle to drive. Robert and I crossed the border in Sumas, Washington, and drove for about two hours when the engine light came on; we were dismayed. I frantically found the manual, which said that we should get it to a garage ASAP, which we did. They told us to go back to Canada to get whatever it was fixed. Poor Robert drove all the way back to Chilliwack, back to the mechanic who had checked the SUV the previous day, and two hours later it was ready to go again.

Now we were way behind schedule, so Robert drove until nearly midnight to catch up. A few hours' sleep in a motel room, and we were off again; we made our rendezvous with Nikki and Lloyd right on time. It was all worth it.

We had a fun time, especially when we were with high rollers and were playing the hundred-dollar machines. That meant lots of free drinks kept coming. Lloyd actually told me to sit down and pull the handle and I won one hundred and fifty dollars! Of course, it all went back in, but it was a thrill; up to that point I'd only played the nickel machines.

We got back in time to go to the hospital in Vancouver, where Sharon was having her third child. Connor was born on March 31, 2002. I was a grandmother for the fourth time. Cara and Stephen were already in Nanton getting settled, and Robert and I traveled there to find a house for us, close to the kids and the bar. The very morning we had arranged to meet a realtor to view properties, Robert and Stephen had a big argument and I had a hard time stopping Robert from heading right back to B.C. He wanted to cancel the whole thing. It was much too late to do that, and I knew it, so I managed to persuade him to look at the nearby town of High River. We found a 1930s house that needed some work but was vacant and priced right.

Robert made several trips in his cube van with our goods. We took some furniture, books, and lots of collectibles. People used to say our house in Chilliwack was like a museum. There was an American bar with one hundred and fifty beer signs, three hundred different beer cans, and a large pool table that we hated to leave behind. The Elvis room was full of memorabilia, a fifties café in the backyard, and a Texaco Station complete with old gas pumps. We had our three big dogs, so Robert made an area in the front of his van for them.

My daughter Joanne kindly offered to ride with me in the Blazer for company and to help us at the other end. We set off in a convoy and stopped halfway at a pet-friendly motel that we had previously booked. Robert, Joanne, me, and three dogs all checked into one room. Robert said very plainly, "All dogs on the floor!" but when he woke early the next morning, Ranger, our Doberman/Labrador cross, was lying splayed across his chest. It was very funny. The next day we made it to High River and another chapter in my life began.

Chapter 12

How to Have Fun and Make Money

Lloyd's Story

Nikki was making plans to go to the antiques fairs in England in April. She wanted me to go to organize the buyers and pick-ups. Julliet, Dom, and Jonathan could make sure that the container was packed. We had a great time at the Brownlow Arms at Hough on the Hill. We would have dinner and drinks with Will and Clare, also with Stephie and Les, and all of the usual gang was there, too. The Brownlow Arms staff was so glad to see that Nikki was in residence!

After working for a week, we traveled down to Gatwick and stayed with Gill and David since they only lived ten minutes from Gatwick Airport. We always had fun with them. We were so lucky to be able to travel to the United Kingdom at least five times a year and stay in contact with all of Nikki's childhood mates.

Nikki and I had built up over a million in sky miles reward miles, so Nikki made sure we bought M. class tickets so we could upgrade to business elite or first class for only forty thousand miles each. We would always from now on travel up front; it is easier to lie down to sleep. Back home, our dog Napier was glad to see us. Ed and Louise came up from Wauchula where they had an orange grove as well as a house on Little Gasparilla Island. Ed said it seemed that April was a good time to be in Blairsville since the woods didn't grow too much in the Florida winters in their orange grove.

Our container came to Blue Ridge the third week of May—just in time for the start of the tourists coming up from Florida for the summer. Julliet and Dom went into a partnership with Tom and Kelly in an antique warehouse in Asheville, North Carolina, where they lived now. They all met the container and hauled away their stuff back to their warehouse. Summer on the lake was so beautiful. We always wanted to live and buy a house there and belong to the Worth/Nottely club where the Wades and Haskins lived with the Jones only one street south, around the edge of the cove. That way we would all be neighbors.

Finally a house on the lakefront came up for sale. It was our friend Scooter's house; she wanted us to buy it for some unknown reason. The house was riddled with termites, but we did not mind. We sold the house on McIntosh and bought her house in October. We were told it had to be torn down because of the termite damage, so we decided to design a new house; and Nikki told Gary, our builder, to be finished by the time we got back in April. She wanted to design the house on his computer. We built a beautiful cracker-style home with a wraparound deck.

We loved it so and stayed there until 2009. Then we sold our dream lake house, closed down the business, and bought a golf course pool home in Placida, Florida, which was close to Little Gasparilla Island where we had spent ten winters in the past. The island was remote with no bridges or roads. Our friends Ed and Louise Sasser would pick us up at the marina and take us to their house for the weekend. They had always loved coming to our lake house and staying with the dogs while we went to England. Then we met Tim and Leslie, who had a house on the Island.

Sometimes in the past, when we were renting on the island, we would have twelve people for dinner parties. Seemed like we were always picking up the children of friends in their boat and bring them over the bay to our dock.

A few years later, Jim and Patricia Monk rented a beachfront house next to ours on the island. The Monks fit right in with all of the island people. We were always at someone's house for sunset or dinner. Ed and Louise and Bob and June both had a house on the bay on Peacock Lane. This was Nikki's favorite lane. George, the grand old man, had a round house on the seafront, and Tommy and Amber's house was next to George's. We stayed at Tommy's for three years. Visitors from England were the Bevans, the McGills, the Sudrons, Aunty Philly, and the Claytons with their delightful granddaughter, Gemma.

Many friends visited Nikki and me for the ten years we were on Little Gasparilla Island, and also my brothers Fred, Mike, and Floyd would come down to fish along with our cousins, the Trimbles. Nikki with her laid-back attitude adapted to the island life, which made her a well-liked person! Nikki's days on the island were full of reading and doing crosswords and shelling. Everything stopped at four p.m. It was time for showers and to get ready for cocktails at five o'clock. We would always talk about our friends and experiences whether it was on the island, Lake Nottley or around the globe. Nothing changed for ten years except regarding June Hicks, who sold her large winter home on Peacock Lane. Nikki really enjoyed June with her family and friends. Many times, June would crank up her boat, the *Sand Witch*, to take us on a Saturday to the Ship's Lantern, a pub and restaurant looking over the Intracoastal Waterway opposite Stump Pass, for Bloody Marys and lunch.

There was absolutely nothing June would not do for us. Her neighbors were the Ridings family, who also had a getaway place on Peacock lane. Later on, June's daughter Judy bought an island home for a weekend retreat on Gulf Street. When June sold her home to move in with her daughter elsewhere on the island, she docked the *Sand Witch* on the bay at the end of Gulf Street and asked us to use the boat to keep it from deteriorating in the salt air. This was definitely a plus for us since the island had no shops or restaurants; we could go fishing, shopping, and out to eat. But Nikki was never bored, and she frequented the little library for fresh books dropped off by islanders. One day, Dr. Dick and Marsha dropped by to see if they could join our group because it seemed we had so much fun! Jerry and Marsha Stead were childhood friends of Taylor and Kathy, who lived on the bay next to the Stokes. They were both retired schoolteachers in Brandon.

The Monks brought a new flavor to the island with Patricia's many boxes of cooking utensils, wardrobes, and their little dog in tow. They had many exquisite dinner parties with wonderful appetizers and very fine wines. Louise Sasser's Southern cooking was always scrumptious; her husband was a look-alike to Jerry Reed, the singer, accent and all. He was a big man who, one could say, really enjoyed Louise's cooking. Then, when Tim and Leslie came onto the scene, well that was another culinary treat. Tim took over many kitchens in people's homes and then provided us all with gourmet meals. Tim's wife, Leslie, was like Nikki— blond, petite, and also from England. Tim and Leslie had met in the Caribbean while working on separate sailing ships. Nikki really enjoyed her walks and talks with Leslie.

We would talk about friends and experiences every day at five p.m. whether it was on the island, at Lake Nottely, or Nikki's beloved Harrow.

Ro's Dad 1980

The quintuplet's fifteenth birthday 1984

Glen Markie Lodge 1984

Ro & John in Hawaii 1986

John, Ro Nikki & Lloyd –Scotland 1986

Ro, Nikki, Julliet & Cara –Florida 1990

Ro & her Dad a month before he died 1992

Julliet's graduation –Lloyd, Julliet, Jonathan & Nikki 1996

Nikki, Lloyd & Ro 1998

Nikki, Gill, Jacque & Ro 1998

Julliet's Wedding 1998

Granny Letts 90th birthday 2004

Nikki & Lloyd travelling first class 2005

Nikki & Ro on the beach Little Gasparilla Island 2004

Nikki & Ro (sitting on the steps of the beach house) 2005

Nikki & Jonathan 2006

Lloyd, Nikki, Ro & Napier the dog on LGI beach 2006

Lloyd & Ro on George's deck, Florida 2012

Chapter 13

The Pub

Ro's Story

The Blacksmith Pub became "Steven's Bar & Grill," a sports bar in a redneck town! The menu was small, but Steven was a good cook; however, his attitude was not as well liked as his cooking. For one thing, he would not allow country music to be played, and that's all some of these cowboys knew. But Cara with her warm personality was an excellent waitress and barmaid and was well-liked by the locals. People were curious to see the new management, so at first business was good, but soon it became more of a struggle to make any money.

We started renovating our house, and poor Ranger was not happy with the move. If a dog can have a nervous breakdown, he had one, tearing up the siding on the house in several places. Robert had to build a wood storage to cover up the worst part. Robert started up his painting business again by putting an ad in the newspaper, but it takes a while in these small towns for people to accept you, so there wasn't much money coming in. My Blazer, which I'd only had six months, broke down in the middle of town, leaking fluid all over the road. I had to have a new transmission put in at the cost of one thousand dollars. I suppose we were lucky that it had made the trip from Chilliwack to Alberta.

Initially the intention was that I should help out in the bar, but having a husband and wife and mother-in-law all working together was not a good idea. I did make the effort a few times, and Cara did her best to help the situation; but it was far too uncomfortable. There was a thrift store at the end of our street, run by the Salvation Army, and after shopping there a few times, I decided that was where I wanted to work, I just got such a good feeling about it. Luckily for me, there was an opening soon after, so I applied, got the job, and absolutely loved working there for the next four years. I met some very good people and made some wonderful friends that would prove invaluable later on.

It was about this time that Tanya was diagnosed with breast cancer. It was a shock, and we were all very worried about her. I was able to talk to her doctor, who sounded optimistic, which helped a lot. She had not been living a very healthy lifestyle; she was the only one of the quints who smoked, and she liked to drink a fair amount, too. Those things coupled with a bad diet and no exercise took their toll. She had the lump removed and then went through chemotherapy and radiation. She has been cancer free ever since. Unfortunately, her lifestyle hasn't changed, and she has had a multitude of other health issues. Through all this, though, her talent shines through and she writes some beautiful poetry and prose.

The winters were so harsh that they were hard to get used to. The big, bright blue sky was a lovely by product of these cold, short afternoons. Many times we would wake up to minus thirties and lower, with the wind chill, to find the windows iced up inside; it was almost like living in an igloo, I imagine. That first spring we had a lot of heavy rain, and water started coming up from underground into the basement; we were bailing all night and barely prevented the water from going into the carpeted bedroom down there, which was half a step higher, thank goodness. I knew now why the town was called High River. The previous flood had been ten years earlier, and luckily there has not been another one since.

The rift between Robert and Steven got steadily worse, and it was constant stress for Cara and me to try to keep the peace. Quite a lot of money needed to be spent on the bar for improvements. It was up to me to spend more of the savings that John had left for me to help in my retirement, and on a place that was uncomfortable to spend time in. We had a cover put on the deck so that there was more seating for the customers, but it rarely filled up.

In 2004, I decided to take Nikki up on her offer to visit her and Lloyd on Little Gasparilla Island in Florida. They had been going down there every winter since 1995 and had invited me so many times; at last I was going! Julliet and Dom met me at the Sarasota Airport; then it was an hour's drive to Placida and then the boat taxi over to the island. Darkness had fallen by this time, and when I walked from the boat ramp to the beach house, I felt like I was walking through a tropical rain forest. There were no roads or pavement, just a white sandy lane canopied by palm trees and large sea grape trees. It was a three-hundred-yard walk from the dock on the bay to a stilt house on the sea. The closer we got to where Nikki was, the more you could hear the rolling surf. I was wondering how my sister-like friend from Harrow had ever found this remote barrier island off the west coast of Florida. I could imagine Nikki more in a posh condominium with a flowing beach dress having a cocktail in the evening, not in a tropical rainforest in the middle of nowhere!

It was wonderful it was to see my good friends again, especially Nikki. When Lloyd and the rest of the family had gone to bed, she and I sat up talking and drinking wine into the small hours. The island was more than I had ever imagined—an endless, white, sandy beach on one side and a beautiful bay on the other. There were very few people, some incredible birds (I especially liked the pelicans), and the most amazing sunsets. My favorite pastime was walking the beach collecting shells and sharks' teeth and paddling in the warm water to the sound of waves breaking. Most sharks' teeth are black, but Nikki once found a large white one. She said it was just there in front of her on the sand. Her aunt Philly had it made into a necklace for her as a thank-you for her stay on the island. Lloyd and I still look for one today, and we've never met anyone else who has found a white shark's tooth on Little Gasparilla beach.

I got to first meet Maisy on that visit. She was Nikki's only granddaughter, a tiny toddler, blond and very cute and adored by both her grandparents, especially her "Baba," as Maisy called Nikki. Today Maisy has the shark-tooth necklace, and I know she will always treasure it.

I loved the island and was mad at myself for not having come down earlier. Nikki and Lloyd had a wonderful social life there, too. Almost every evening there were drinks at sunset at somebody's house, and often dinner get-togethers, eating mainly fish that had been caught that day. One morning, I was walking the beach and Lloyd was casting his net. It looked like something straight out of the Bible. I remember him saying to me, "Isn't this a wonderful life here?" and I agreed. How I missed John and wished that he could have experienced this.

**

That year, in July, Granny Letts, John's mother, had her ninetieth birthday. His brother, Geoff, was planning a family party for her at his home in Langley. The whole family was going, so Robert and I thought it would be a great trip and an opportunity to see all of the kids at one time, which didn't happen often anymore. It was an excellent party, and Granny was very happy to have the family together. The following June we gathered there again for Joanne and Brian's wedding. Geoff and Di had a beautiful yard, and it was a perfect setting. Joanne looked lovely; it was another happy day to treasure.

The following November on the 16, 2005, Joanne gave birth to a lovely baby boy, Cooper. Brian had a seven-year-old daughter from his first marriage - Delaney. I was a grandmother of six now, and that is where it remains. I don't believe that Tanya or Gary will ever be parents. Just before Christmas 2005, my lovely Cousin Rosalind died in England of multiple sclerosis at age sixty-one. She had battled it for many years, and it just became too much for her to live with in the end.

I had always known that Robert had fathered a child when he was seventeen. Earlier in our relationship, he had made a couple of small attempts to find her. It had made me feel a little nervous because I knew he always acted in haste and repented at leisure. I would not have tried to stop him, but I was glad when he put it to the back of his mind. One day during our third year in Alberta, there was a call from his sister in Ontario. His daughter, called Cheryl, had at last found her mother after many months and now wanted to contact him—there was a phone number to call. I knew in my heart that everything was about to change.

They talked for an hour on the phone; then the next day, he bought an airplane ticket to Ontario. I helped him pack all his best clothes, and he was gone for two weeks. He came home with tales of a wonderful reunion with Cheryl and her eleven-year-old son, Mathew. From all of the photos he had taken, I could see there was a strong family resemblance. The photos were promptly framed and put on the sideboard. A few days later I accidently found real estate information from Thor, where Cheryl lived. Robert confessed that he was making plans to move there, and he hoped that I'd understand that he'd been waiting for this to happen for twenty years. I did understand, up to a point. Our marriage had suffered mainly due to the stress over the bar and also over the fact that his temper often got out of control.

Robert told me all he needed was a relatively small amount of money to get started, and so I went to a lawyer to get the papers dawn up. He packed his cube van full of as many of his collectibles as he could fit in, and just two days before he was due to leave, a letter arrived for him. I could see that it was from Cheryl. If only I hadn't given it to him! I thought about it for a moment, but of course, I had to. It was a heartbreaking letter for Robert; Cheryl basically told him not to come to Ontario. She also said she could not condone him leaving his wife—me—and that she and Robert should let things cool right down.

Foolishly, I let Robert stay. For a while I think he tried to treat me better, but the underlying problems were all still there. It's true what they say: the more things change the more they stay the same. Steven and Cara thought even less of him now, so things were even more awkward. The bar was not making any money; it was just hanging on by a thread, and Steven and Cara were getting deeper and deeper in debt. The situation was not good for their daughter, Jade, either.

My friends at the Salvation Army were very supportive and understanding throughout this traumatic time. Karen Franson in particular was wonderful. She was a great cook, a single mother, and would often cook extra food for Robert and me so that I wouldn't have to cook supper when I got home from work. Most of us who worked at that thrift store seemed to have personal problems of one kind or another, but we all were always there for each other. It was a very special place.

A block down the road from where we lived was an animal rescue organization run by Kim Hessel from her home called "Heaven Can Wait." Soon after we had moved in, I went down there to volunteer for walking dogs. Every week I'd walk one or two dogs for an hour. One I remember was a Pyrenees crossed with a wolf; his name was Chewy, and he was a gentle giant much bigger than me who thankfully got adopted after a couple of years there. I loved it, even though I heard some horrible stories about some of the rescues.

One of the dogs I was asked to walk was a little shepherd-cross pup called Fig. He was the runt of the litter found on a reservation with his siblings and a starving mother. They had all been adopted except for Fig; one of his legs had not developed properly so he was a little crippled. He had a beautiful face with stand-up ears and wonderful eyebrows. I fell in love with him and offered to foster him. We already had three dogs so I couldn't straightaway adopt him; it would be a little too much—not for me but definitely for Robert.

One day while walking the dogs off leash by the river where I always went, Patsy, our springer spaniel mix, ran off and did not come back when I called her. I finally found her eating a deer carcass that was very decayed. She got very sick, and we couldn't save her even though we tried everything; we had to put her out of her misery. By this time Robert had grown fond of Fig, too. We now called him Figgy, and with Robert's OK I asked Kim if I could adopt him and she was delighted.

Not long after, Robert and I had a huge argument about the bar and money. He said that the dogs were costing too much and that the last one in would be the first one out. He added that I would not want to know how he would get rid of Figgy. I took this as a threat on the life of my dog, and without a second thought, I called the police. They came to the house, and as soon as Robert gave them a piece of his mind, they handcuffed him and took him away. He spent a night in jail and was very remorseful by the next day, but I don't think he's ever completely forgiven me for that.

The police and everyone else advised me not to have Robert back. He came with a police escort to get his clothes and personal belongings, and I felt strong and confident that I could deal with all of this. I got lots of support from Cara and Steven and my friends at work. Robert found an apartment close by. I'd see him going to the launderette, which was across the road from the thrift store, and I'd feel quite sorry for him.

In less than two months, I had weakened and Robert had talked his way back into my life. This was to be a costly mistake, but I took the marriage vows very seriously and thought I should give it one more chance. Steven was furious with me, and we have had a strained relationship for years because of it. Nikki, of course, was always on my side whatever decisions I made, but I knew she thought taking Robert back was a bad one, and she was right, of course.

However, we made every effort to make the marriage work. Lloyd had told me the last time I was on the island to bring Robert the next time. Nikki called me one day in November to say that they had more Delta points than they could use, so they would like to fly us down for a holiday on the island. It would be much quicker than driving!

The following January, we flew to Tampa, rented a car, and Lloyd met us at a Publix grocery store and took us over to the island in his flat-bottom boat. I loved being back there and seeing Nikki again, but Robert quickly got bored. There was not enough action for him, as he was not a reader or a fisherman, so after a few days, we left to tour some other parts of Florida. We came back to the island for a few days before heading back to the cold winter in Alberta.

Cara and I knew that the situation with the bar was getting critical. It had limped along for almost three years. We were all losing money, so we agreed to try to sell it. It was very difficult with Robert and Steven not talking at all at this point, and several real estate people wouldn't touch us when they saw the situation. By some miracle, Cara found a buyer, but we had to lower the price quite a bit. We took the matter over from the men and got it signed, sealed, and delivered before they could object. I was going to miss my daughter, but I was happy that this stressful situation was over and she and her family could make a fresh start. They chose the town of Comox on Vancouver Island, and they still live happily there today.

Nikki called me almost every week at five p.m., but this particular day the call was much earlier. When I heard her voice, I knew something was wrong. They'd had to have Napier, their beloved black lab, put down; his back end had gone. We shared a love of dogs, and she knew I would understand. We cried together; I loved that dog, too, even though I'd only seen him a few times. I got some other bad news in 2006. Kathy, our old neighbor in Surrey, had died of liver cancer at just sixty years old.

Without the bar to worry about, life was a little better. Robert was getting enough painting work, and our house renovations were about done. I was still enjoying my job at the Salvation Army. Early one morning, there was a knock on the door; two of my friends and coworkers Karen and Coleen had come to tell me that the store had burned down during the night so there was no need to go in that day! But it's amazing what can happen when people work together. Within a week we were in a new temporary location with tons of donations. Three youths were later charged with arson. The oldest one got ten years in jail.

Our fifth Alberta winter arrived, and going south in the New Year really helped to break it up. Nikki and Lloyd had moved into a new house in Hudson, Florida, so we thought we'd drive down to see them. Somehow we crossed the border at the wrong crossing; it was in the early hours of the morning, but we still wondered why no one else was there. On the other side, we suddenly found ourselves on twisting roads of black ice with no barriers.

Thank goodness Robert was a very skillful driver or else we would not have made it. I was petrified with fear until we got on the proper road; then I thanked my guardian angels again for looking after us. It was a bad January in 2007 weather-wise in many US states. We had to alter our route several times but could not escape it altogether. In Oklahoma, we spun in a complete circle between two eighteen-wheelers due to black ice, and landed mercifully unscathed in a ditch. As it was shallow ditch, we actually managed to drive ourselves out. Thank goodness we had a four-wheel drive vehicle. All the way through Texas it was torrential rain, so we were very happy when we reached

Florida. The angels, we feel, wanted us to make it to Hudson in one piece.

We finally made it into Florida after two weeks of winter driving, and started peeling off clothes. Nikki and Lloyd were out on the deck when we arrived. It was so great to see them! Their new home was a lovely house on a canal looking out over the Gulf of Mexico. Nikki's cousin Pete and his wife, Anne, were there, and that evening, Lloyd took us out on his flat-bottomed boat into the Gulf. We drank champagne and ate oysters; it felt like the lifestyle of the rich and famous! Nikki and Lloyd always knew how to enjoy themselves. We toured around the area during the day enjoying the small beach towns nearby, but we were always back by five p.m. for drinks!

Nikki and Lloyd's son, Jonathan, lived in Asheville, North Carolina, and they heard he was in some kind of trouble. Whenever he needed her, his mother was always there. Nikki left for Asheville so it was time for us to leave to make our way back to Alberta.

It was a long drive home, and I always looked forward to seeing the dogs again. They stayed at an excellent kennel, which was part of the "Heaven Can Wait" organization where Figgy came from. The new next-door neighbor was watching our house, and she seemed very nice. We took her back a heron purchased from a garden shop in Florida for her yard as part of a thank-you gift, along with some wine. She said she liked it very much and all was well.

A few weeks later, Robert got upset when she hired another painter to paint her house outside, and some unpleasantness resulted. The next day, when we came home from Calgary, the heron was lying in the middle of our back yard. She'd evidently thrown it over the fence!

Robert was furious and immediately got a hammer and nailed the heron on top of the fence between our properties for all to see. He had already fallen out with the neighbors on the other side, so now no one was speaking to us.

On my sixty-first birthday, my friend Karen gave me a beautiful glass swan dish, and I put it on the coffee table. Later that week, in the evening, Robert had had a few drinks. Normally he was in a better mood with a drink inside him, but this particular night something upset him, and he must have felt it was my fault because he picked up the glass swan and smashed it to smithereens! He told me he was not going to clean it up, and I said that I certainly would not. As I took the dogs and went downstairs to the bedroom in the basement, I realized that I could not put up with Robert's bad temper anymore. The next day Robert did clean up the mess and was sorry, but the damage was done in more than one way.

**

After Cheryl's letter rebuking Robert and returning all the gifts he had given her, including an emerald ring, his reaction was to angrily wipe her out of his life again. He destroyed all of the pictures of her and Mathew and every other reminder of the reunion. A few months later, he softened and wrote to her again. I suppose she was feeling a bit guilty, who knows, but she replied and they started keeping in touch again; then Robert bought an airline ticket for his grandson to come and spend two weeks with us. I made every effort to give Mathew a good time. They took my SUV and went off on several sightseeing trips. I even went with them on one occasion and bought Mathew a small gift as a souvenir, but I found Mathew to be a very precocious thirteen-year-old who listened to rap music with obscene language content. So I was quite relieved when he went home.

The next morning, Robert took my Blazer out for the day and blew the engine. The SUV was towed home, and I was a little upset, to say the least! Luckily, I could walk to work. Robert wanted us to buy a new car, but I knew our marriage was on shaky ground, and I did not want to get involved in owning a vehicle together; the Blazer was just in my name. The mechanic called me at work to tell me the price of a new engine; it was a lot of money but he said the car was worth it. Now I know better, but that day I told him to go ahead.

When I got home from work that evening and told Robert, he went ballistic! It was the last straw, I suppose, and he told me he wanted out of the marriage, just like that. This is what I had wanted for quite a while, but I needed him to be the instigator; otherwise he could have gotten very nasty. He had once told me that if I ever wanted a divorce, he would take me for every penny I had and make my life hell. Now that he had patched things up with his daughter, Cheryl, I knew he would want to move there again although he had not actually come out and said it.

I knew him pretty well by this time, and I had to think quickly. Then a plan came to me. Robert was a very impatient man, so I offered him one hundred thousand dollars to leave as soon as possible. I would take care of selling the house and everything else. That was about one-third of what the house was worth, but in Alberta things don't automatically get divided down the middle in a divorce. After a little negotiating, Robert agreed to $110,000 and all his collectibles. I went to a lawyer and got a legal separation drawn up. Robert had to get his own lawyer, of course, but he signed everything quickly and easily; therefore there was no holdup. I felt so energized at this point; it was just all go, and there was no hesitation or second-guessing. Robert had to be gone within two weeks, and I needed to help him pack. There were three hundred die-cast cars to be packaged in their original boxes, which took days. Also there was all his Elvis memorabilia, Texaco and cowboy collections, and of course, his most treasured beer signs; they all had to be packed up carefully. He was forced to leave behind a lot of the less-valuable ones and the hundreds of beer cans (every one different), which took years to collect and I just took to recycling later.

We were amazingly civil during this time. It was as if we both knew that our time together had run its course and we were moving on to new lives. Finally the cube van was packed right to the very top. I remember crawling in there, just below the roof, to push one more thing in—I was much smaller than Robert—and so with check in hand, he kissed me good-bye and Robert drove away. I haven't seen him since and have never looked back. We decided to stay friends; what's the point in being anything else? After all, we'd been together nineteen years and shared some good times as well as bad, and I knew that he had a lot of good in him. I wished him well knowing it was going to be easy for him to start up again in Ontario.

Thank goodness for friends, I could not have gotten through the next six weeks without them. I listed my house with the daughter of my manager at the thrift store and it sold within a week. Property was at its peak at this time; a month later it started to drop. I got an offer after the first showing, so the house never even got on the Web site; it was incredible! The buyer also wanted to buy all of the antique furniture, which was a bonus. I think John was looking after me in some way. I felt so much positive energy; everything just seemed to be falling into place.

My friend Dee took me to the airport, and I flew to Comox where my daughter, Cara, met me. I had only three days to find a house for my two dogs and me because the closing date was only a month away!. I had been in contact with a realtor online, and he met us in Chemainus to show us properties he'd lined up. I needed to have a fenced yard and be fairly close to town, as I would need to find work.

We saw many uninteresting houses with little or no character; then, halfway through the second day, we found the perfect place, an older home that had been tastefully renovated with a lovely tiled floor. I made an offer, and by the next day it was accepted. It was so good to have Cara with me to make such a big decision, and I felt very confident about it. I flew back to Alberta knowing where my next home would be.

With the help of my friends at the Salvation Army, I had a garage sale three weekends running, and what was left went to the thrift store. After work and on days off, there was always someone to help me pack, I was so grateful for all the kindness. Finally it was my last night in High River. As always I took my three dogs out into the back yard before bedtime. Suddenly Ranger collapsed; something was wrong with his back legs. I somehow got him inside, gave him some baby aspirin, and lay with him all night. By the time morning came I knew what had to be done. I called Colleen and Karen, and Colleen's husband, Glen, brought his truck over. We got Ranger on a blanket, each of us held a corner, and we got him into the truck and took him to the nearest vet. I held Ranger until it was over, crying my heart out. I think he just did not want to move houses again and was satisfied with his twelve happy years.

I was now running about three hours behind to make it to the motel I had booked at the halfway point of the journey. The Blazer was loaded, Cody was on top of a pile in the back, and Figgy was squeezed in the front. I put *The Secret* in the CD player—by chance, a virtual stranger had given it to me—and set off for British Columbia. We made it to the pet-friendly motel, and the dogs and I enjoyed some dinner and well-deserved rest. The next morning we hit the road again, drove over the mountains, and made it to Geoff and Di's place in Langley by late afternoon. That day, the Coquihalla—the long mountainous highway I had just driven—had its first snowfall of the year. Considering it was the last day of September this was hardly surprising. How lucky was I to miss that! Someone again was certainly looking out for me on another very long, arduous drive.

That night heavy rain started falling, and in the morning with it still pouring down, Cody, Figgy, and I set off on the last leg of the journey. As I got to the ferry at Horseshoe Bay, the attendant told me that it would be a three-hour wait because I wouldn't get on the first ferry. Since I had been listening to *The Secret*, I did not let that get me down, despite two dogs in a packed car and it pouring down with rain; I knew it would be OK, and it was: I was the very last car let on the first ferry.

When I got to the Travel Lodge in Nanaimo I was somewhat amazed and very thankful that they let me in with two drenched dogs. I felt I had made it. The following day I moved into my new house, so happy to be independent and living in a much warmer part of Canada. Cara, Joanne, and my son-in-law, Brian, who grew up in Nanaimo, came over. He knew where everything in town was and how to get there and was a big help. To top it all off, Nikki called to say congratulations; she was very happy that I was free of Robert.

Chapter 14

Maisy Is Finally Here

We went to Julliet and Dom's house in Boone, North Carolina, for Christmas in 2002. Jonathan was joining the family, and Julliet's baby was due at any time. Dominic deep-fried a turkey for Christmas dinner. Julliet, Dom, and Jonathan opened up their stockings, one of the highlights of the holiday. Nikki had taken hours to hide a hundred-dollar bill, a fifty-dollar bill, a ten, and a five in all the stockings; she would take toys or small tools apart to hide the money in. The larger the bill, the tougher it was to find; we always loved Christmas Eve and Christmas Day.

Boone was icy cold and snowy, and taking our dog, Napier, a large black Lab, for a walk several times a day gave me respite from being cooped up. We were all getting on each other's nerves except Nikki because she could not wait for our first grandchild to be born. But New Year's Day came, and we were still waiting. I decided to drive down to Florida to our place on Little Gasparilla Island. It was a big relief to be on my own for a few days. I love LGI! A few days later, Nikki called to say, "Your granddaughter was born in a blizzard, a beautiful little girl, and her name is Maisy!" It was January 6, 2002.

I surprised everyone by walking in the door four days after on January 10. Julliet cried with joy when I walked into her bedroom. I could hardly believe my eyes: how small her baby was! Nikki was beaming because her daughter had a little girl. Maisy was definitely the apple of Nikki's eye!

After a few days Nikki, Napier, and I took off. We stayed the first night in north Daytona, and when we woke up the next morning it felt so good being in Florida. We packed up, took a cup of coffee with us, and just drove, enjoying the warm weather and the beauty of the Florida seaside. A Daytona police officer pulled me over for going ten miles over the speed limit. I was so mad that I told Nikki I would never go to Daytona, Florida, ever again; to this day I always avoid Daytona Beach.

We arrived at Eldred's Marina in the early afternoon, Ruthy was very glad to see us. She always had a big, beautiful smile. We had reservations with the water taxi for two p.m. We had to shop for everything including jugs of water for the dog. Since the well was only five feet deep on the island, the water was brackish and smelly, mainly used for the toilets. We bought enough provisions for ten days; there was bottled water, gallon jugs of water for us to drink for coffee and tea, and plenty of food and snacks. We would unload on the dock, walk to the house, open it up, and Nikki would go up the stairs. The house was on stilts. I took the golf cart back to pick everything up and would make many trips up those stairs lugging everything in, then Nikki would put it all away. We both were so excited to be on the island again!

As soon as five o'clock was on us, and we took our drinks and the dog in golf cart to George Geier's round house on the beach front on Peacock Lane. The Sassers were there; Louise said, "You finally made it!" and Ed said, "Oh, brother, Louise, it's time to go to our home in Wauchula!" Dick and Laura were also there, and George was all smiles when he saw us, a great start to our four-month stay. On our way back to our place, we did a small detour by Judy Thome's house. Judy was there with her mom, June Hicks from Peacock Lane. They were really lovely ladies. They invited us all in, the dog as well. They had three dogs. We had a nice visit, and June asked me to use their boat again this year as it would be better than storing it while they were not on the island.

George was now eighty-eight years old. He called me up wanting to go over on the boat with me to shop for groceries. I took the golf cart to George's dock so I could help him with his shopping. George had taught me how to throw the cast net to catch mullet; now we were always eating mullet! The first year Jacque and David were on the island, we were on George's dock and had caught twenty large mullet. Jacque started filleting with us; I was very surprised she could do it, being a lady from Harrow on the Hill.

**

By 2004, Juliet, Dominic, and Maisy were in Asheville, North Carolina, with their antique partners, Tom and Kelly Haskins. Julliet said to them in July, "We are going to Mom and Dad's lake house in the Georgia Mountains—it's Lake Worth Nottely Club." Tom was laughing, saying "My parents, too, have a place on the same circle!" It turned out we were neighbors to Jim and Caroline Haskins; they all came to the lake for the Fourth of July celebration. This was also when the association would have their AGM. Julliet often left Maisy with Nikki so that she and Dom could boat and water ski with all of the Haskinses on Lake Nottley. Well, Nikki tried to keep up with Maisy, but our granddaughter was a challenge. She could run and crawl faster that Nikki could follow her, trying to protect her from falling from any edge. Every morning Maisy joined Nikki and me in bed for storytelling. Nikki loved this, as Maisy was her pride and joy. I would then have to get up and make the tea.

October came quickly, and we were off to Little Gasparilla Island again. We both loved crossing the Florida line; it always felt so right. The next day we were on the island—hooray! We soon settled in and got back to island life, with George making sure that we would be on his deck at five p.m. The following week it all happened again; we were either at a party or staging one, usually twice a week, and having sunset cocktails at George's house.

Julliet, Dominic and Maisy arrived on December 20. What a Christmas it was going to be! The next day, Nikki took Maisy on the beach. Her tiny feet were sinking into the sand, and she could not understand how this was happening. Jonathan arrived on Christmas Eve. It was good being all together again especially, as we never knew if Jonathan was going to show up. Sometimes he would stay with his friends to party and we wouldn't hear for him for days on end.

Christmas Day arrived with presents and stockings. Nikki and Maisy were propped up in bed while Dom and Julliet slept in. I was the tea boy that morning for everyone. It really wasn't a chore when I could listen to the waves. The Gulf of Mexico was just outside our screened in porch. Julliet and Dom would be slowly waking for a cup of tea with the smell of bacon cooking whiffing through the house. Jim Monk was stirring next door; he took their dog Annie down to the beach, and I let Napier out to join them; of course, Annie started barking, and then you could see the lights in the other houses coming on and people coming to life. Julliet, Jonathan, and Dom ambled out to the living room by nine. The feeling was excited anticipation!

We all started to set up for the traditional turkey dinner Nikki was preparing. That Christmas, George and his sister-in-law, Gussy, joined us for dinner. Gussy arrived about three p.m., and we had a sherry waiting for her out on the front porch. We were all trying to spot a dolphin like always. Soon the waters were churning with dolphins herding mullet; they pushed thousands of mullet toward the shore, and we all ran down to watch. Gussie said, "Lloyd, go get your net," and Jonathan ran back to the house to fetch it from the golf cart. Julliet by this time was in the water with the dolphins. She said the mullet kept running into her legs there were so many! I threw the net and caught three large, roe-laden mullet; they were on their way to spawn way out into the Gulf. The mullet was for Gussie— her Christmas present to take back to her rented beach home on Peacock Lane. We wanted this day to last forever.

Once the children and grandchild left, we started getting ready for the Bevans. They were going to rent Judy's house for six weeks. We had to hang the hammock so David could read and take his naps in the afternoon. Jacque and Granddad would fish every day either from the boat or on the shore. We picked them up at the Sarasota/Bradenton airport in the middle of January. It was so good to see them again; we probably have spent more than twenty holidays with them over the years, in France, Scotland, Spain, England, Portugal, or Florida. The years never changed: Nikki and David were still listening to Jacque and me arguing our political points. Our spouses always had to tell us to leave it alone so we all could do something together.

**

In the summer of 2006, Julliet and family came to the lake several times. Maisy was always on the bed with Nikki by six thirty in the morning watching TV or playing Baby Einstein. I always was the one to make tea for my little girls. Julliet and Dom would sleep until eight a.m. They were either at the Wades or the Haskinses the night before socializing. During the day they would water-ski then go off to the warehouse on Saturday to off-load the forty-foot container full of antiques. We all shared expenses, shipping, and customs duties.

In 2007, we again had the Bevans family, and Jim and Jeanette came over from Scotland. That winter we had lots of visitors from the UK plus Lee and Jimetta Anderson from Tampa. Nikki was in her element, doing the *Daily Telegraph* online crossword, reading, and visiting. When we came back from fishing or grocery shopping, the rule was everyone had to be showered and dressed for drinks at five o'clock.

That winter, Ro and Robert came in from British Columbia for a week. Ro and Nikki talked a lot and walked along the beach looking for sharks' teeth or neat-looking shells. Robert was getting bored doing nothing, so he talked Ro into leaving to explore more of Florida. Nikki never forgave him for cutting Ro's time short on the island by a few days.

We rented Judy's house for six weeks for extra guests. Mostly it was Jacque and David and their son and daughter-in-law, Mez and Paula. Meredith on the first day fished too long in the surf and his legs were sunburned. We cut open several aloe leaves to soothe the burning and to also repair damaged skin cells.

Nikki loved everyone dropping by, bringing their own favorite drinks. June and Judy loved their bottles of gin and tonic. The ladies always helped with the cleanup at dinner parties or whatever. Leslie and Jacque were the ones to wash and dry, with Louise scraping dishes. The men talked about their latest fishing trip or the Gulf temperature being right for the kingfish moving down south or migrating north towards Texas.

Chapter 15

On My Own

Ro's Story

Work was a little harder to get now that I was in my sixties, but because of my experience, I was hired by the Salvation Army to work in their thrift store in North Nanaimo. As it turned out I did not enjoy the job near as much as I had in Alberta. The management was very domineering, and I was made to feel like a naughty schoolgirl many times—a feeling I thought I had put behind me. Traps were set to catch us, like giving in-need customers a discount or putting things on hold for people or letting volunteers buy goods before they had been on the floor enough time—silly little rules that to me were not compassionate. Our breaks were timed almost to the second, and it was frowned on if we talked too long to a customer or a fellow worker. However, my coworkers were wonderful women who made the days bearable, and we all worked there only because needed the income.

I was most upset to hear about David Clayton's battle with cancer. Nikki kept me constantly updated, and I was very saddened when I heard that he had died in February of 2008. Granny Letts died soon after on March 3. She would have been ninety-four the following July. A few weeks later, the whole family gathered for a memorial at John's grave in Surrey, British Columbia. Geoff scattered his mother's ashes around his brother's grave. She wanted to be with her son. It was a sad day for the family, losing the last grandparent.

My daughter Cara knew I was not happy at work, and so she was always encouraging me to do something I loved, which was to look after dogs. I was a little scared to take the plunge and quit my job to start a small business at home; but something happened that gave me the push I needed. One November morning in 2008, I noticed my six-year-old dog, Figgy, was not well. He had been drinking more than normal but otherwise seemed fine. Over the next few weeks, Figgy needed to go for several tests—all to no avail, unfortunately. I was told to take him to a special animal hospital in Vancouver as soon as possible. The situation was critical.

It was close to Christmas and the store was getting busy so I was not very popular with my boss. Joanne, my daughter, kindly said she would stay over and look after my other dog, Cody. There was snow on the ground, and Figgy and I froze in the car on the front of the ferry over to the mainland. Two days later we were back home; there was still with no diagnosis but there *was* a sizable bill. I could not leave him; every day he got a little worse. The vet said it must be a brain tumor as everything else had been ruled out.

On Boxing Day, my local vet came to the house and gave Figgy an injection; he passed peacefully away. I remember that waiting for the vet to come was excruciating. I listened to Irish music while I stroked my sick dog. After, I called Nikki, and we cried together as we had when Napier, her dog, had to be put down. All the kids called; they were all very concerned and caring, as were all of my friends. Everyone had loved Figgy, too.

Some people say they could not have another pet after going through such hell, but I felt differently. Even with my lovely Cody, there was a huge gap where Figgy had been. I did go back to work the next day, but soon I was looking online at all the dogs needing a good home through the SPCA and many other adoption agencies. One day I was on the Victoria Adoptables Web site and saw this little fellow looking at me over the screen. I knew he was the one for me, so I did the application online right away and it was accepted.

This sixteen-week-old husky mix had been found by a nurse who regularly went into a Native American reservation in Port Hardy to rescue dogs. He was in extremely bad shape with a broken pelvis and other injuries. The vet said he'd been suffering at least two weeks with the broken bones. Central Mountain Air flew him south to Victoria where he was taken to Victoria Adoptables, treated by a vet in town that gives his services free, and nursed back to health by Carol Broad, the owner of the rescue organization. This little fellow made a remarkable recovery. One of the stipulations on the adoption form was that he could not be left alone for at least two months. So the next day I told my boss that I would not be returning to work after the next Saturday. On that Sunday, my daughter Joanne, my son-in-law Brian, and my grandson Cooper, drove with Cody and me down to Victoria and got the new addition to the family. I called him Rosco, which means "from the deer forest." My son, Gary, was living in Victoria at that time, working for a car rental company, so we met for lunch and went for a lovely walk along the cliffs.

Figgy is in my heart forever, but getting Rosco really helped me with the grief. Now I was forced financially to get some income, so again encouraged by Cara, I put an ad online offering a doggy day-and-night care service. The response was immediate, and I kicked myself for not having done it sooner. I charged less than other dog-care businesses and was often told that I should raise my prices, but I hated taking money from people when I so enjoyed looking after their dogs and a lot of my customers became new friends. I was fortunate to have a big, fenced yard and a suitable vehicle that would accommodate up to five dogs, and so I could take them out for lovely long walks.

During this time, I met my good friend Jill and her dog, Goldy, along with another friend, Anne, with her dog, Sadie. They both lived close by and would often help me with my many dogs—it really was a lot of fun. We'd walk, rain or shine, and when I had several soaking-wet dogs to clean up, I felt I earned every penny I made.

The kids always loved visiting because they never knew what dogs I would have at home, and we are a family of animal lovers. Nikki was very supportive of my venture—she still called me every week and filled me in with what was happening. My life seemed very tame compared to hers, and I loved hearing about their great social life and the properties they were buying and selling. She always ended the converstion with "love you loads". She said that every time to all her family and friends and meant it a hundred percent.

In July of 2009, I lost my darling Cody to cancer. Thank goodness I had Rosco, but this time, because of the business, I decided to stick to just one dog. Unfortunately, another doggy day care owner reported me to the town council for not having a license. Therefore I had to get a license, which costs the same whether you are a one-woman operation or a multimillion-dollar company; it doesn't make any sense. Then I had to get extra insurance, which I shopped around for to make it even feasible to operate. It was still all worth it; I was my own boss and I loved my doggies. I was never lonely and did not miss Robert at all. I was feeling quite content and was sure that men were out of my life for good!

Cara, Steven, and Jade were still enjoying life up in Comox on the east coast of Vancouver Island, and Cara was really making a name for herself as an artist. She worked five nights a week managing a restaurant, and once a year, she displayed her art there. Several pieces always sold; one picture got auctioned twice for one thousand dollars each time. She had several commissions, too, and the future was looking bright. Steven started "Street Smart Kidz," which teaches kids to become street smart through classes, a Web page, and DVDs. Jade, my beautiful granddaughter, who had grown into a tall and lean beauty, loved her schoolwork and was very athletic.

Joanne, Brian, and Cooper lived the closest to me, and I'd see them quite often. I was delighted to get to know Cooper better; like his parents, he had always been a great little hiker and we had some wonderful walks together. Gary came up occasionally to visit from Victoria, and it was always good to see him; he was then working at another car rental place. Tanya lived close to Cara in Comox at this time with another boyfriend who sounded less than ideal. She still had a number of health issues, mental as well as physical, and kept to herself quite a lot. Sharon, Darin, and their three kids were still living happily up in Quesnel, seven hundred miles north of Vancouver. Unfortunately, the only time I got to see them was when they came down for Granny's ninetieth birthday in 2004 and then again for her funeral in 2008.

In October 2009, my childhood friend Daphne called to say she'd been diagnosed with breast cancer. She had the operation in November and started chemotherapy soon after. She had lost her mother at ninety-five the January before, and they had just sold the house she'd been born in. She and Alan moved to Seaford Sussex in January 2010, and Daphne continued her chemo there. Today she is clear of cancer, thank God, and is enjoying a full life with her family and her church.

Christmas 2009 saw me looking after five dogs as well as Rosco. I always talked to Nikki over Christmas, and she sounded her usual vivacious self. But early in January 2010, she called me, and there was a serious tone to her voice: she told me that a pap test she'd had showed probable cervical cancer. A couple of weeks after that, she called me again, telling me it was confirmed. I was shocked and concerned. There was some good news, though; the tumor was small, and there was every probability that the cancer could be cured. I immediately made plans to go to Florida. It was not an easy journey—twenty-three hours—but so worth it to see my friend again.

We had many talks sitting beside the pool; we called all our friends and discussed the possible treatments. At that time, Nikki was planning to have chemo as well as radiation, so we went shopping for hats. Because she had a small head, most of them would have been too big with none of her lovely blond hair. So, we resorted to scarves. Needless to say, we had lots of laughs along the way despite the seriousness of it all. I cut her hair pretty short, as she thought that would make losing it easier. She was being both practical and positive, although she eventually decided not to have the chemo.

I did notice that her energy was low, and she held one hand on her back as though she had a backache. Lloyd was stoic as always, wonderfully supportive; in fact, he had originally made the doctor's appointment for her, as she was very reluctant to do so. One day, when Nikki and I were out by the pool talking about her forthcoming treatments, we decided to call Daphne, who had just gone through chemo herself.

Daphne was very encouraging, telling Nikki that the treatment was not as bad as she had expected. It was a different cancer she was battling, but the conversation helped Nikki a lot. One day, all three of us drove around the neighborhood looking at properties for sale. They were all so cheap that I toyed with the idea of selling my place in Nanaimo and buying in Florida—just to live there six months. I'd have money leftover, but where to live for the other six months of the year? It did get me thinking about what to do next.

When I said good-bye to Nikki that March day in 2010, I did not allow myself to think that I would never see her again, but that was how it was going to be. That whole summer we talked on the phone a lot, and my heart bled when she told me about some of the treatments she was going through, never complaining and extremely brave.

I was back to my business of dog care, and then one day I had a problem with a husky that I'd thought was OK behaviorally. Suddenly, he bit the ear of a sweet St. Bernard puppy called Sophie. Blood was spurting, I was frantic, and my heart was pounding. I put the husky in the garage and did first-aid on Sophie. Luckily the wound was not too serious and the owners were very understanding, but I could have had a major problem if they were going to show or breed that dog. It was a sign that I should again change my lifestyle. I started looking at cheaper places to live and came across Little Qualicum River Village. It seemed too good to be true, and it was only fifteen minutes from Qualicum Beach. After further investigation my friend Jill, who was also thinking of moving, encouraged me to go and take a look. We drove up there one day with all our dogs, and by the time we got back, I had bought a one-year-old little rancher, subject to selling my house in Nanaimo. Property was not selling easily at that time in Nanaimo, but the universe was on my side; my house sold for a good price in two weeks! Figgy's Diggs, as I had called my business, had closed its doors for good.

Qualicum Beach is a quaint little town on the east coast of Vancouver Island, much sought after and quite expensive, but fifteen minutes away is this lovely development on four hundred acres next to a beautiful provincial park with huge waterfalls and a rushing river. Because of the distance from town and the zoning being recreational, property is priced a lot lower. Yet all of the homes are less than ten years old. Mine is on an acre, and you can hear the river as you lie in bed.

It is beautiful in the Village, surrounded by mountains and trees; there are bears, deer, and even the odd cougar, although I've never seen the latter. It's a great place for a dog, and Rosco loves it. Jill and her dog, Goldie love it too. She bought a place up here a month after me, so I still have my walking companion when I'm there and a house minder when I am not. My kids all came to see the new place and thought it was great. Nikki said it sounded lovely and that she and Lloyd were happy for me, as were all of my friends. Some were amazed at the speed of my decisions.

When Nikki's breathing became a problem, we had to curtail the phone calls. In the end, they could only be two minutes in length, and I'd e-mail Lloyd to arrange a time.

The radiation had killed the cancer but had brought on COPD and aggravated her osteoporosis.

I talked to Lloyd and said that I wanted to come down to see Nikki and help any way I could. I didn't know for sure that she was terminal, but he did and told me to come as soon as I could on Nikki's airline points. I agreed, and he booked my flight for March 1.

Julliet, their daughter, signed up with Caring Bridge, which is a Web site where you can leave a message for someone who is sick and read other people's messages, too. Nikki read them every day in bed on her laptop. In the end she had over one thousand messages. Julliet posted updates every day about how her mom was doing. Every morning I would rush to the computer to read them. Some days were good, others not so good. The morning of February 22, I read, "Mum died yesterday." My heart stopped, and I felt like I'd been hit hard in the chest. I started crying and hardly stopped for two days. Apart from calling my kids and Jill, I could not see or talk to anyone. The third day I got myself together and realized life must go on, and I e-mailed Lloyd and Julliet.

Should I still fly down? The points for my ticket had been used and could not be given back, and the funeral would already have passed by March 1. I called Lloyd, and he told me I could postpone the trip until the fall, but what would be the point, I wondered. We decided I could help him sort some of Nikki's clothes; she wanted me to have any that I wanted so I agreed to go. I didn't know how I was going to feel. Lloyd met me at the Tampa airport; it was very good to see him but so strange without Nikki. When we got to the house, I could almost feel her still there. It was good and almost comforting to feel her presence.

Leslie, their friend from the island, who has now become my friend, came the following day to help me sort the clothes. Instead of it being a sad and morbid job, we made it fun, and Lloyd said he could hear us laughing. He liked that. Leslie read all the sympathy cards to Lloyd, as he hadn't been able to do it himself. We all then made plans for Nikki's memorial on the island. Lloyd's cousin Larry came to the house, and we all went over to Little Gasparilla Island in the flat-bottomed boat.

Leslie and her husband, Tim, have a very nice house on the island called the acorn house because of its shape. They offered to put me up there, and I wasn't sure what to do. Lloyd and Larry were going to stay in George's round house right on the sea's edge, and that was where the get-together for Nikki was taking place that evening. He had died a few years ago in his nineties and the house was now in the hands of his family. They were kind enough to let friends stay there. There was room for me there, too.

Everyone on the island who knew Nikki came at drinks time, five o'clock. They each came with a dish and a cocktail. It was a celebration of her and her love of life. Quietly grieving, Lloyd, without any of us knowing, scattered Nikki's ashes on the sand beneath the deck and said good-bye to the woman he loved. After everyone went home and cousin Larry had gone to bed, Lloyd and I sat out on the deck in the dark with the sound of the waves lapping over Nikki's ashes below.

There had never before been any hint of romantic feelings between us before, but that night something happened; we both felt this sudden connection that neither of us had planned or expected. The next day, Lloyd took Larry back to the mainland and came back to me on the island. For four days we clung to each other in grief and for comfort. Lloyd was distraught, and although he was putting a brave face on it, at times he would fall apart completely. He knew that I had been through that desperate, unbearable grief; and holding on to me helped him through the darkest days of his life. Maybe Nikki knew that I would be there for him and I think she would want two of her favorite people together.

The situation was a little difficult. Nikki's death had only been two weeks ago. It was all too soon, but how do you time something like this? I went back to Canada with these very strong emotions. We could say nothing to anyone. Lloyd had to go to Nikki's memorial in England. I would have loved to go for Nikki's sake, but I knew it would have made the day more difficult for Lloyd and he needed to say good-bye on his own.

No one will ever replace John for me or Nikki for Lloyd; we both loved them both so much, and we will share that together forever.

Chapter 16

My Darkest Days

I am winding down this tribute to Nikki. Our last two years were to be full of anxiety, darkness, and hurt. We thanked God that our lake house sold for a lot of money. I wanted to buy on LGI, but Nikki liked a house across from the island on the mainland in Cape Haze. The house was on a golf course with a large swimming pool, all screened in, and a huge master suite—all on the ground level.

This was August 2009. We both loved this house on Arlington Drive, number nine. All the neighbors were delightful, and they invited Nikki and me to all types of parties. Phil and Alison Hill, both English, live across the street on Coral Creek, which leads out to the Intracoastal Waterway, and then into the Gulf of Mexico. They stay there for six months then visit family for one month in the UK and five months in Spain. We had quite a few meals and five o'clock drinks with them. As it turned out, this house was another good move. Even though we did not know, of course, that my darling was going to be diagnosed with cancer, this house on Arlington Drive was to be an excellent place for her to recover from forty days of radiation.

Early in January 2010, Nikki was diagnosed with cancer. She took the lead with her own health decisions, interviewing doctors, clinics, and herbalists. She decided she was not going to have chemotherapy but was going to take the forty treatments of radiation. During these treatments, Nikki was rundown and became infected with a chest cold; that eventually developed into COPD. Her breathing deteriorated in the coming months, and she had to have to have oxygen tanks and breathing apparatus. By Christmas, Nikki was struggling.

Thank God again, during this year, Nikki had visitors from England—they came to see her and loved being with her without knowing how sick she was; many were friends from Nikki's childhood in Harrow, including Jacque and David, Ed and Lyn, and Ro from Canada. Many friends from Florida would come to stay: Lee and Jimetta, Ed and Phyllis and my brother Floyd and his wife, Marlene. Nikki's cousin Pete Frost and his wife, Anne, along with their son, Julian, came from England and were a welcome diversion for her. Julliet, Maisy, and Dominic also came over from England, and Jonathan came down from Asheville, North Carolina, several times to see his mother. Our dear friends Jeff and Kathy from Atlanta came and saw Nikki two weeks before she left us for the other side. Kathy and Nikki spent quite a while, just the two of them, talking. Nikki told me later how much it meant to spend these times with her friends and family from over three countries!

Julliet, Maisy, Dominic, and Debbie and Kevin Diggle and their son Matt were here for Christmas in 2010 when Nikki was rushed into the hospital on Christmas Eve. The ambulance was called when Kevin, Matt, and I were on the golf course. We hurried home to see Nikki on her way to Englewood Hospital. Julliet and I followed. Nikki was so breathless that they transferred her to a larger hospital in Port Charlotte. Lots of friends showed up to see her, but only Jimetta, Phyllis, Julliet, and I were allowed in to see her. Oh, how we all cried in the hallway, and one of the doctors came out to comfort us. We still had Christmas dinner for Maisy, who was just seven years old—Nikki's main reason for living, our only grandchild. She was such a polite, pretty, petite little girl, so sure of herself, and Nikki absolutely adored her.

Nikki stayed in Fawcett Memorial Hospital for the next five days, and then she was transferred to the large pulmonary hospital in Sarasota on December 29. I followed the ambulance with Nikki's personal items and went to see her settled in that morning; I kissed her and told her I would be back that afternoon. I went home and walked Polly the dog, who knew that something was very wrong; she would always be lying beside the bed when Nikki was at home. After a nap I went back to the hospital, taking with me a bottle of chardonnay with a corkscrew and a wine glass for Nikki's five o'clock cocktail. She could barely drink one glass, but what a little treat for her. Julliet had bought Nikki a small laptop computer so that she could read her e-mails every day, and she also set up Nikki's Web page on the Caring Bridge site. During the next seven weeks, Nikki would get 1016 e-mail messages—it was astonishing how popular she was!

The doctors told me that Nikki only had a few months to live. I instructed all them not to tell Nikki because she was so optimistic about recovering. One day I came home weeping and lay down on the bed. Polly, who knows never to do this normally, jumped up on the bed beside me. She wanted to comfort me.

Nikki wanted to go home after being in Sarasota for seventeen days, but the doctors told her she had to get her breathing down under ten units before she would be allowed. On January 19, 2011, she managed it. Hospice set up all of the equipment in our bedroom on the twentieth, and on the twenty-first, Nikki came home. HOORAY! We were so very happy! Marlene, Floyd's wife, came over to help. She lived with us, staying in the same room with Nikki for seventeen days. I did all the cooking for the three of us. After that, I asked Marlene to go home and get some rest because I would like to take over caring for my Nikki. For the next two weeks, I would do it all. How I loved her, and I kissed her many times every day, all the time wondering, as I still do, *Oh, God, why did this happen to her?*

All through this time, Nikki was optimistic. We talked about various treatments and even looked in to a lung transplant. We made plans about what we would do when she got better. I never let her know what the doctors had told me. Julliet, Maisy, and Dom arrived on February 16. On the twenty-first, Julliet was sitting in the chair by Nikki's bed, and Nikki told her, "I can't do this with you staring at me." She had made a decision. We called the hospice nurse, Heidi, and she arrived shortly after. She instructed me to get the kit out of the fridge, and she gave Nikki her morphine. I went in to see Nikki after Heidi came out, and I put the Bible next to her and we held hands on it. I read the twenty-third psalm, and Nikki passed away; my duchess was gone forever except in my mind and on my lips. I thank God every day for me being with Nikki for forty-four years.

We had the funeral the next week in Tampa at Lee and Jimetta's church. Nikki wanted to be cremated. Friends of ours from all over were arriving at Tampa's Church of God. There was a sheriff's car and a Tampa police car provided by J.R. Burton, a major with the Sheriff's Office. J.R. and his family were friends of ours from Hudson. Pastor Ron was easy to listen to. I had the bagpipes play "Swing Low, Sweet Chariot" and Nikki's favorite song, "Morning Has Broken." Julliet and Jonathan handled everything as well as they could. Sadly they had laid their mom to rest and said their good-byes.

I went back to the house in Placida by myself. Polly was to be my listening ear—I did talk to Polly. I also talked to Nikki that night. I e-mailed Ro to please call me. She had lost her loving husband and my good friend in 1987, also after taking care of him at home, so she would understand and know what to do. Ro called within fifteen minutes; she listened while I cried for over an hour. We both hung up our phones and then slept for a while.

Ro was due to fly into Tampa in two days; she had hoped to see Nikki one last time, but she called me to say that she had second thoughts about coming down. I said I understood, but I thought Nikki would have wanted her and Leslie to go through the clothes and shoes before sending them off to the Humane Society Charity Shop. I told her that it would be a big help to me, so Ro came down to Florida and I met her at the airport. A few days later we went over to LGI, and I privately scattered Nikki's ashes over the sandy beach beneath George's deck, where Nikki had spent so many enjoyable evenings. That was her wish—to be on the sands of the Gulf of Mexico. That Friday night there were a dozen friends gathered together to wet down Nikki's ashes. We celebrated her life with us.

That week was traumatic. I was so consumed with grief. Ro held on to me for four days until the worst was over, then went back to Canada. Julliet was trying to put together a memorial in England, and the next week, she called Laurie and Bob, Nikki's cousins, to tell them about it. Those two guys were like brothers to Nikki, and they said they wanted to organize Nikki's tribute. It was to be the third week of March in the village of Fornham St. Martins near Bury St. Edmunds. The wake would be at the pub across the street from Laurie and Donna's house. So it was settled; they organized the whole thing, and Julliet posted the details on the Caring Bridge Web site.

I called Laurie to see if the vicar would allow Nikki's vicar from St. Luke's Episcopal Church in Blue Ridge, Georgia, to assist in memorializing Nikki. Laurie called back the next day saying that the other vicar had agreed. I flew over to England a few days later to stay with Julliet in Sheffield before driving over to Fornham that Friday. I was dreading another gut wrenching episode, but how wrong could I be! It was a beautiful event, especially the church with flowers arranged by Donna and her family—yellow flowers to match Nikki's memorial brochure. All of the ladies looked radiant, and the men were dressed in suits, looking handsome. Maisy looked gorgeous—Nikki was so proud of her. Nikki's picture sat on the altar, and the sun shone through the stained-glass window right onto the photo, giving her an aura. Those who saw it said it was amazing! The sun made the village glorious, and the church was overflowing. What a tribute to be surrounded by Nikki's family and friends.

It seems like for forty-four years, I have been either traveling to Nikki or with her. After saying good-bye to my beautiful wife in Fordham St. Martins, I was a body in a fog, lost among voices of comfort in the dark from many family members and friends. I must add that our son, Jonathan, was not at the memorial because of my concern with the wake being in a pub. Being surrounded by sympathy and good intentions may have been too much for him. Cousin Bob told me that Jonathan should have attended, and looking back to how beautiful the celebration of Nikki was, I could have been wrong.

There are so many wonderful life stories and enjoyable experiences that I have not mentioned in this book. There are lots of sagas yet to be told. It is time to end this one for now and say thank you to my Nikki, Ro's John, our lovely late friends John Holder and Dave and Ed Clayton, and all our other relatives and friends too numerous to mention at this time.

Speaking for myself, being a part of the Harrow on the Hill group, I will be forever indebted to Nikki for introducing me to her world and most grateful to Nikki's friends for accepting this country boy from Florida.

Thank you, my darling, my duchess, for all you have given me—two beautiful children and a wealth of acquaintances that would last for half a century.

Your Loving Squeak,

Lloyd

Epilogue

Losing Nikki was the end of my normal everyday life, then Ro arrived soon after on Nikki's airmiles. Ro helped me through the darkest time when it was so difficult to see even into the next hour. After Ro left to go back to Canada, I missed and needed her. There was something brewing between us. I felt comfortable in our close relationship to the point of planning a trip to England together, to visit Harrow and old friends, as well as visits to British Columbia where Ro lives.

Printed in Great Britain
by Amazon